EMPOWERED FINANCES

Empowered Finances

A Guide to Financial Freedom for Moms

TAYLOR CALHOUN

Illuminated Ideas Publishing

Contents

Chapter 1

Chapter 1: Introduction

Welcome to "Empowered Finances: A Guide to Financial Freedom for Moms." I'm thrilled you've picked up this book, and I want to extend a warm welcome to all the incredible moms out there who are navigating the challenging yet rewarding journey of managing finances on their own.

In this chapter, we embark on a journey together, exploring the fundamental concept of financial independence. As moms, we wear many hats – from being the household CEO to the nurturing heart of our families. Amidst the joys of motherhood, we often find ourselves facing unique financial challenges. Whether you're a single mom, a working mom, or a stay-at-home mom, this book is crafted with you in mind.

Our exploration begins by understanding the true essence of financial freedom. What does it mean to have control over our finances, and how can it empower us to create the lives we envision for ourselves and our loved ones? We'll delve into the significance of financial independence for moms, recognizing that our financial well-being is intricately linked to our ability to provide a stable and secure environment for our families.

Throughout this chapter, we'll candidly discuss the common financial hurdles faced by moms – from budget constraints to navigating through unexpected expenses. It's essential to recognize these challenges as the first step towards overcoming them. This book is not just about managing money; it's about reshaping our mindset, empowering ourselves, and building a foundation for a financially fulfilling life.

So, whether you're a new mom seeking financial guidance or a seasoned pro looking to refine your money management skills, this chapter sets the stage for the transformative journey that lies ahead. Get ready to embark on a path of self-discovery, financial empowerment, and the realization of your dreams. Together, we'll navigate the world of money with confidence and build a brighter, more secure future for ourselves and our families. Let's dive in!

Understanding Financial Independence

Welcome to the first chapter of "Empowered Finances: A Guide to Financial Freedom for Moms." In this section, we embark on a meaningful exploration of the cornerstone of our financial journey: understanding financial independence.

Financial independence is not just a buzzword; it's a concept that holds the key to unlocking the doors to the life you dream of. Let's start by envisioning a life where money isn't a source of stress but a tool that empowers you to make choices aligned with your values and aspirations.

At its core, financial independence is about having the freedom to make decisions without being solely constrained by monetary considerations. It's the ability to live life on your terms, whether that means pursuing a passion, providing for your family, or planning for the future without the constant weight of financial worry.

Now, let's break it down a bit. Financial independence is not necessarily about having vast wealth or being completely debt-free. It's about achieving a state where your financial resources align with your life goals, providing a sense of security and peace of mind.

Think of it as having a financial safety net that catches you when life throws unexpected curveballs. Whether it's a sudden medical expense, a home repair, or an exciting opportunity you want to pursue, financial independence allows you to navigate these situations with confidence rather than trepidation.

For moms, understanding financial independence takes on a unique significance. It means being able to create a stable and nurturing environment for your children, offering them opportunities for growth and education. It's about being the guiding force in their lives, free from the constant worry about financial constraints.

Financial independence also affords you the flexibility to make choices that align with your values as a mom. Whether you choose to stay at home and focus on your family, pursue a fulfilling career, or strike a balance between the two, financial independence provides the foundation for these choices.

As we delve deeper into this concept, it's important to recognize that financial independence is a journey, not a destination. It's a gradual process of building habits, making informed decisions, and adapting to life's changes. It's about learning to navigate the ebb and flow of financial challenges with resilience and a sense of empowerment.

Throughout this book, we'll explore practical strategies to cultivate financial independence in your life. From budgeting and saving to investing and planning for the future, each chapter is designed to guide you through the steps that contribute to your financial well-being.

So, let's embrace the journey of understanding financial independence. It's not just about money; it's about reclaiming control over your life, fostering a sense of security, and creating a future where you have the freedom to live the life you've always envisioned for yourself and your family. Let's embark on this transformative journey together.

DEFINING FINANCIAL FREEDOM

In our quest for financial empowerment, it's crucial to begin with a clear understanding of the foundation – defining financial freedom. So, what exactly does financial freedom mean, and how does it play a pivotal role in shaping the course of our lives?

At its essence, financial freedom is the state of having the resources and flexibility to make choices without being hindered by financial constraints. It's the ability to live life on your terms, pursuing your passions, and making decisions that align with your values and goals. Think of it as having the financial bandwidth to say 'yes' to opportunities and 'no' to things that don't resonate with your vision.

Financial freedom is not a one-size-fits-all concept. It varies from person to person and is deeply intertwined with individual aspirations, lifestyles, and circumstances. For some, it may mean having enough savings to cover living expenses for an extended period, providing a sense of security and peace of mind. For others, it could involve generating passive income streams, freeing up time to focus on personal or family pursuits.

As moms, defining financial freedom takes on a unique significance. It's about being able to provide for your family's needs comfortably, without sacrificing quality time with your loved ones. It's having the financial stability to weather unexpected challenges, ensuring a secure environment for your children to thrive.

Beyond the practicalities, financial freedom is also about reclaiming control over your time. It's the freedom to choose how you spend your days – whether that involves pursuing a career you love, dedicating more time to family, or engaging in meaningful hobbies. It's the liberation from the constraints that financial stress can impose on our daily lives.

It's important to note that financial freedom is not synonymous with extravagance or excessive wealth. It's about achieving a balance between your income, expenses, and the life you want to lead. It involves making intentional choices about where your money goes, aligning your spending with your values, and understanding that true wealth goes beyond the numbers in your bank account.

Moreover, financial freedom is an ongoing journey rather than a final destination. It's a process of continuous learning, adapting to life's changes, and making informed decisions along the way. This journey involves building healthy financial habits, setting realistic goals, and embracing the mindset that financial freedom is attainable through gradual progress.

Throughout this book, we'll explore practical strategies to help you define and attain financial freedom in your life. From budgeting techniques to investment strategies, each chapter is designed to provide you with the tools and insights needed to navigate the path toward financial liberation.

So, as we embark on this journey together, let's embrace the notion that financial freedom is not just a distant goal but a present reality we can cultivate in our lives. It's about taking charge of our financial destinies, shaping a future filled with choices, and living a life that reflects our true priorities.

THE IMPORTANCE OF FINANCIAL INDEPENDENCE FOR MOMS

Delving deeper into our exploration of financial independence, let's shine a spotlight on why this concept holds such paramount importance for moms. Beyond being a personal aspiration, financial independence for moms is a cornerstone that not only impacts individual lives but also ripples through the entire family dynamic.

To grasp the significance, let's consider the multifaceted role of moms. Moms are the heartbeat of the household, juggling myriad responsibilities with unwavering dedication. From nurturing the emotional well-being of their children to managing the practicalities of daily life, moms are the linchpin that holds everything together.

Financial independence, for moms, is like a sturdy foundation upon which this intricate tapestry is woven. It provides a sense of security, a safety net that catches the family when unexpected challenges arise. Imagine the peace of mind that comes from knowing you have the financial resources to navigate through life's twists and turns without compromising your family's well-being.

One of the primary aspects of financial independence for moms is the ability to provide a stable and nurturing environment for their children. It's about more than just covering the basics; it's about affording opportunities for growth, education, and enrichment. Financial independence empowers moms to invest in their children's futures, ensuring they have the tools and support needed to thrive.

Moreover, financial independence enables moms to make choices that align with their family values. Whether it's deciding to stay at home and dedicate more time to family or pursuing a career that fulfills personal aspirations, financial independence provides the flexibility to make these decisions without the constraint of financial stress.

The importance of financial independence for moms also extends to the realm of role modeling. Moms are powerful influencers in their children's lives, and the way they approach finances shapes their children's financial attitudes and habits. By demonstrating the value of financial independence, moms instill in their children a sense of responsibility, resourceful-ness, and a proactive approach to managing money.

Furthermore, financial independence safeguards moms against the vulnerabilities that may arise due to unforeseen circumstances. Whether it's a sudden health issue, a change in employment, or other unexpected challenges, having a solid financial foundation allows moms to navigate these situations with resilience and confidence.

It's crucial to recognize that financial independence doesn't imply going it alone. Instead, it's about having the autonomy to make choices collaboratively and to contribute meaning-fully to the family's financial well-being. Moms play a pivotal role in shaping the financial landscape of their households, and achieving financial independence empowers them to do so with confidence and purpose.

As we navigate through the various facets of financial in-dependence in the chapters ahead, keep in mind that this journey is not just about money; it's about creating a life that resonates with your values and aspirations. It's about being the best version of yourself for your family and laying the groundwork for a future filled with possibilities. Together, let's continue exploring the transformative power of financial in-dependence for moms.

COMMON FINANCIAL CHALLENGES FACED BY MOMS

In our journey toward financial empowerment for moms, it's essential to acknowledge and understand the common financial challenges that many mothers face. While the path to financial independence is undoubtedly rewarding, it's paved with hurdles that, when addressed with insight and resilience, can lead to transformative change.

One prevalent challenge is the balancing act between work and family life. Moms often find themselves navigating the delicate equilibrium of pursuing a career while also being the primary caregivers for their children. This dual role can pose challenges in terms of time management, as moms strive to meet both professional obligations and the ever-present demands of family life.

Inconsistent or unpredictable income is another hurdle faced by many moms. Whether due to fluctuations in work hours, freelance income variability, or irregular employment, the uncertainty of income can make budgeting and financial planning a complex task. This unpredictability can lead to stress and financial strain, making it challenging to build a stable financial foundation.

The cost of childcare is a significant financial consideration for moms, particularly for those who are working outside the home. Quality childcare can be expensive, and the associated costs can sometimes offset a significant portion of a mom's income. This creates a dilemma, as moms weigh the financial implications of working against the desire to provide the best care for their children.

Single motherhood introduces its own set of financial challenges. Managing the household and raising children on a single income can be financially demanding, often requiring single moms to be resourceful and strategic in their financial decisions. From housing to healthcare, single moms face the responsibility of shouldering the financial needs of the family on their own.

Debt is a common financial challenge that many moms grapple with. Whether it's student loans, credit card debt, or other financial obligations, managing and repaying debt can be a significant stressor. Balancing debt repayment with other financial goals, such as saving for emergencies or investing, requires careful planning and commitment.

Emergencies and unexpected expenses are a reality of life, and moms are often tasked with navigating these financial surprises. Whether it's a medical emergency, car repairs, or home maintenance, the financial strain of unexpected costs can disrupt carefully crafted budgets and pose challenges in maintaining financial stability.

Lastly, there's the challenge of financial literacy. Many moms may not have had the opportunity to receive formal financial education, leaving them to navigate the complex world of personal finance on their own. Understanding terms like investments, retirement accounts, and insurance can be daunting, but building financial literacy is a crucial step toward achieving long-term financial independence.

Acknowledging these challenges is the first step toward addressing them. In the chapters that follow, we'll delve into practical strategies and insights to navigate these obstacles, offering guidance on how to build resilience, make informed financial decisions, and ultimately achieve the financial freedom that is within reach for every mom. Together, let's explore the transformative journey toward financial empowerment and overcome these common challenges with confidence and determination.

Chapter 2

Chapter 2: Mindset Shift

Welcome to Chapter 2 of "Empowered Finances: A Guide to Financial Freedom for Moms." In this chapter, we dive into the transformative power of a mindset shift – a journey that transcends numbers and budgets to explore the incredible impact our thoughts and beliefs have on our financial well-being.

Our mindset, or the way we perceive and approach money, is a powerful force that shapes our financial reality. In this exploration, we'll unravel the layers of our money mindset, challenging any limiting beliefs and embracing a growth-oriented perspective. Because, beyond the dollars and cents, lies a world where our attitudes towards money play a pivotal role in unlocking our true financial potential.

Consider this chapter as a mirror reflecting the relationship between your thoughts and your financial outcomes. We'll navigate through the intricacies of overcoming limiting beliefs – those subtle whispers that may have held you back from realizing your financial dreams. It's time to release any notions that may have tethered you to a scarcity mindset and open the door to the abundance of possibilities that financial freedom can bring.

Embracing a growth mindset is the cornerstone of our journey in this chapter. It's about fostering a mindset that sees challenges as opportunities, mistakes as lessons, and believes in the capacity for continuous learning and improvement. As moms, this mindset shift is not just about finances; it's a holistic approach that can permeate every aspect of our lives, influencing how we approach challenges and seize opportunities.

We'll explore how building confidence in financial decision-making is intertwined with our mindset. Trusting your instincts, setting achievable financial goals, and envisioning a future of abundance are all integral parts of this mindset shift. It's about understanding that you have the power to shape your financial destiny and cultivating the self-assurance to make decisions that align with your vision for yourself and your family.

So, let's embark on this journey together – a journey that goes beyond spreadsheets and account balances. It's a journey of self-discovery, empowerment, and the realization that by shifting our mindset, we hold the key to unlocking a world of financial possibilities. Get ready to challenge old beliefs, embrace new perspectives, and pave the way for a mindset that propels you towards the financial freedom you deserve. The canvas is yours, and the mindset shift is the brush – let's paint a vibrant picture of financial empowerment together.

Cultivating a Positive Money Mindset

As we embark on the journey to cultivate a positive money mindset, let's explore the profound impact our thoughts and beliefs have on our financial well-being. Your money mindset is like the lens through which you view your financial world, influencing your attitudes, behaviors, and ultimately, your financial outcomes.

Cultivating a positive money mindset begins with awareness. Take a moment to reflect on your current beliefs about money. Are there any negative narratives or limiting beliefs that may be holding you back? It's okay if there are – acknowledging them is the first step towards transformation.

One common limiting belief is the scarcity mindset, which tends to focus on what we lack rather than what we have. It's the voice that whispers, "There's never enough," or "I'll never get ahead." Recognizing and challenging this mindset is crucial for cultivating positivity. Shift your perspective to one of abundance, acknowledging the resources and opportunities that surround you. This shift opens the door to possibilities and encourages a more optimistic approach to financial decisions.

Another aspect of cultivating a positive money mindset involves reframing your relationship with money. Instead of seeing money as a source of stress or restriction, view it as a tool for creating the life you desire. Money becomes a means to achieve your goals, support your family, and contribute to the things that matter most to you. By embracing this positive perspective, you empower yourself to make financial decisions aligned with your values and aspirations.

Gratitude plays a vital role in fostering a positive money mindset. Take a moment each day to reflect on the financial aspects of your life that you are grateful for. It could be the ability to provide for your family, the support of a reliable income, or the opportunity to save for future goals. Expressing gratitude shifts your focus from what you lack to what you have, creating a mindset of appreciation and abundance.

As moms, our mindset not only shapes our financial reality but also sets an example for our children. Consider the messages about money that you're passing on to the next generation. Cultivating a positive money mindset in yourself becomes a gift to your children, teaching them healthy financial attitudes and habits that will serve them well in the future.

Building confidence in financial decision-making is a natural outcome of a positive money mindset. Trusting your instincts, setting realistic financial goals, and celebrating your financial victories, no matter how small, contribute to this confidence. Remember that mistakes are part of the learning process, and a positive mindset allows you to view them as opportunities for growth rather than setbacks.

As we progress in this chapter, keep in mind that cultivating a positive money mindset is an ongoing practice. It involves consciously choosing your thoughts and challenging any negativity that arises. By doing so, you're not just transforming your relationship with money – you're creating a foundation for financial empowerment that will positively impact every aspect of your life. Embrace the journey of cultivating a positive money mindset, and let the transformation begin.

OVERCOMING LIMITING BELIEFS

Let's delve into the profound task of overcoming limiting beliefs in our pursuit of a positive money mindset. Limiting beliefs are like invisible barriers that can hinder our financial growth and prevent us from realizing our full potential. Recognizing and challenging these beliefs is an essential step towards cultivating a mindset that empowers rather than constrains.

Often, limiting beliefs stem from early experiences or societal conditioning, shaping our perceptions of what is possible or permissible in the realm of money. Take a moment to reflect on any beliefs you may hold about money, success, or your own financial worth. Are there any messages that tell you, "I'm not good with money," or "Financial success is only for others, not for me"? Identifying these beliefs is the first step towards dismantling their influence.

One prevalent limiting belief is the notion that financial success is reserved for a select few or is inherently tied to luck. This belief can create a sense of resignation, leading to a passive approach to financial matters. It's essential to challenge this mindset by recognizing that financial success is attainable through intentional efforts, learning, and perseverance. Shift your focus from external factors to your own abilities and choices, acknowledging your capacity to shape your financial destiny.

Another common limiting belief is the fear of failure or making mistakes with money. This fear can lead to hesitation in making financial decisions, causing missed opportunities for growth. Embracing a positive money mindset involves viewing mistakes as stepping stones to success rather than insurmountable obstacles. Each financial decision, whether successful or not, contributes to your financial learning journey.

The belief that money is the source of all problems can also be limiting. While financial challenges are a reality, viewing money as inherently negative can create a mental block towards financial empowerment. Shift your perspective by recognizing money as a tool for achieving goals, supporting loved ones, and creating positive change. This reframing allows you to approach financial decisions with a sense of purpose and positivity.

As moms, it's common to encounter limiting beliefs related to balancing family responsibilities with financial pursuits. The belief that focusing on one aspect compromises the other can create internal conflict. Challenge this belief by recognizing that achieving financial success as a mom involves finding a balance that aligns with your values. It's not about choosing one over the other but creating harmony between your family life and financial goals.

Overcoming limiting beliefs requires a conscious effort to reframe negative thoughts and replace them with affirmations that support your financial aspirations. Affirmations can act as powerful tools in this process, helping to reshape your mindset. Repeat positive statements about your financial capabilities and worth regularly to reinforce a positive money mindset.

Remember, the journey to overcome limiting beliefs is ongoing. Be patient and compassionate with yourself as you navigate this process. Surround yourself with positive influences, seek support when needed, and celebrate the progress you make along the way. By challenging and overcoming limiting beliefs, you're not just transforming your mindset – you're unlocking a world of possibilities where financial empowerment becomes a reality. Keep embracing the journey of self-discovery, and watch as your positive money mindset flourishes.

EMBRACING A GROWTH MINDSET

Now, let's explore the transformative power of embracing a growth mindset in our journey toward financial empowerment. A growth mindset is a perspective that sees challenges as opportunities, views failures as stepping stones to success, and believes in the capacity for continuous learning and improvement. Cultivating a growth mindset in the realm of finances opens the door to a world of possibilities and propels us towards achieving our financial goals.

At the core of a growth mindset is the belief that our abilities and intelligence can be developed through dedication, learning, and perseverance. When it comes to finances, this mindset shift involves recognizing that our financial knowledge and skills are not fixed but can evolve over time. It's about embracing the idea that, regardless of your starting point, you can learn, adapt, and make informed financial decisions that contribute to your financial well-being.

One aspect of embracing a growth mindset is reframing failures as opportunities for growth. In the context of finances, setbacks or mistakes are not viewed as indicators of incompetence but as valuable lessons that contribute to your financial learning journey. Instead of dwelling on past financial missteps, a growth mindset encourages you to extract lessons from those experiences and use them to make more informed decisions in the future.

A growth mindset also involves seeking out challenges rather than avoiding them. In the realm of personal finance, this means actively engaging with financial concepts that may initially seem complex or intimidating. Whether it's understanding investment strategies, budgeting techniques, or financial planning, a growth mindset prompts you to approach these challenges with curiosity and a willingness to learn.

Continuous learning is a fundamental aspect of a growth mindset. In the ever-evolving landscape of personal finance, staying informed about new trends, tools, and strategies is key. This doesn't mean you have to become a financial expert overnight; rather, it involves adopting a mindset that values learning as an ongoing process. Stay open to new information, explore resources, and consider seeking advice or guidance when needed.

As moms, embracing a growth mindset in our approach to finances sets a powerful example for our children. Demonstrating resilience in the face of financial challenges, showcasing a willingness to learn, and emphasizing the value of growth and improvement contribute to shaping a positive financial attitude in the next generation.

Moreover, a growth mindset instills a sense of empowerment. It fosters the belief that you have the ability to shape your financial destiny and that setbacks are not permanent roadblocks but temporary detours on the path to success. It encourages a proactive approach to financial decision-making, where you actively seek out opportunities, set realistic goals, and take intentional steps toward financial well-being.

In the chapters ahead, we'll delve into practical strategies and insights to nurture and sustain a growth mindset in your financial journey. Remember that embracing a growth mindset is not about perfection; it's about progress and the commitment to continuous improvement. By adopting this perspective, you're not just transforming your relationship with money – you're opening yourself up to a world of financial growth, empowerment, and the fulfillment of your financial aspirations. Embrace the journey of cultivating a growth mindset, and watch as it becomes a guiding force on your path to financial freedom.

Building Confidence in Financial Decision-Making

Let's explore the essential aspect of building confidence in financial decision-making, a skill that forms the bedrock of a positive money mindset. Confidence in managing your finances is not about having all the answers; it's about trusting your instincts, making informed choices, and understanding that you have the capacity to navigate the complexities of personal finance.

First and foremost, building confidence involves recognizing and celebrating your financial victories, no matter how small. Did you successfully create and stick to a budget for the month? Did you contribute to your savings, even if it was a modest amount? Acknowledge these achievements as milestones on your financial journey. By recognizing your successes, you reinforce the belief that you can make positive financial decisions.

Setting realistic financial goals is another key component of building confidence. Instead of overwhelming yourself with grandiose objectives, break them down into smaller, achievable steps. Whether it's saving for an emergency fund, paying off a credit card, or starting an investment portfolio, setting clear and realistic goals provides a roadmap for your financial journey. Achieving these goals, one step at a time, boosts your confidence and motivates you to tackle more significant financial milestones.

Trust your instincts when it comes to financial decision-making. You possess a unique understanding of your financial situation, goals, and values. While seeking advice and information is valuable, don't underestimate your own intuition. Trusting your instincts involves tuning into your financial needs, assessing the available options, and making choices that align with your values. Over time, this practice contributes to a sense of empowerment and confidence in your ability to make sound financial decisions.

Educate yourself about personal finance. Building confidence is closely tied to knowledge and understanding. Take the time to learn about basic financial concepts, investment strategies, and budgeting techniques. Familiarity with these topics not only demystifies the world of finance but also equips you with the tools to make informed decisions. Consider reading books, attending workshops, or seeking advice from reputable financial sources to enhance your financial literacy.

When faced with financial decisions, take a proactive approach. Avoid procrastination and indecision, as these can erode confidence. Embrace a mindset of problem-solving and view financial decisions as opportunities to learn and grow. Remember that not every decision will be perfect, but each one contributes to your financial experience and understanding.

Surround yourself with a support system. Building confidence in financial decision-making is not a solitary journey. Seek advice from trusted friends, family members, or financial professionals. Share your financial goals and challenges with someone you trust, and consider joining online communities or forums where you can learn from others' experiences. Having a supportive network can provide valuable insights, encouragement, and a sense of community as you navigate your financial path.

Lastly, be patient with yourself. Building confidence in financial decision-making is a process that takes time and practice. Understand that there will be ups and downs, and mistakes are part of the learning curve. Approach each financial decision with a growth-oriented mindset, viewing challenges as opportunities to refine your skills and enhance your confidence.

By focusing on these aspects – celebrating victories, setting realistic goals, trusting your instincts, educating yourself, taking a proactive approach, seeking support, and practicing patience – you lay the foundation for building confidence in your financial decision-making. Remember, confidence is not about being flawless; it's about embracing the journey, learning along the way, and gradually developing the assurance that you can navigate the world of personal finance with confidence and competence.

DEVELOPING LONG-TERM FINANCIAL GOALS

As we continue our exploration of building confidence in financial decision-making, let's delve into the crucial aspect of developing long-term financial goals. Long-term goals serve as the guiding stars of your financial journey, providing a sense of direction and purpose. They empower you to make decisions aligned with your aspirations, laying the groundwork for a secure and fulfilling financial future.

Long-term financial goals are like the blueprints for your dreams. They extend beyond the immediate concerns of today, reaching into the horizon of your future. These goals give shape to your vision – whether it's purchasing a home, funding your children's education, or enjoying a comfortable retirement. Developing these goals is not just about numbers on a spreadsheet; it's about creating a roadmap for the life you want to lead.

Start by envisioning your ideal future. What does financial success look like for you? Picture the aspects of life that matter most – from your family's well-being to personal fulfillment. This exercise helps crystallize your long-term aspirations, providing a foundation for setting meaningful financial goals.

When developing long-term financial goals, consider the different dimensions of your life. Financial stability is not isolated from other aspects such as health, relationships, and personal growth. Your goals should reflect a holistic vision that encompasses both financial objectives and the broader spectrum of your well-being. By integrating these dimensions, you create a more comprehensive and balanced set of long-term goals.

Ensure that your long-term goals are specific and measurable. Instead of vague aspirations, such as "save for retirement" or "buy a house," break them down into tangible, achievable targets. For example, you might set a goal to contribute a specific amount to your retirement fund annually or save a certain percentage of your income for a down payment on a home. This level of specificity not only makes your goals more actionable but also allows you to track your progress over time.

Consider the time horizon for your goals. Long-term goals typically extend over several years or even decades. Understanding the time required to achieve each goal helps you establish a realistic timeline for your financial planning. It also allows you to allocate resources and make strategic decisions in alignment with each goal's timeframe.

Flexibility is key when developing long-term financial goals. Life is dynamic, and circumstances may change. Be open to reassessing and adjusting your goals as needed. Periodically review your progress, celebrate achievements, and make modifications based on shifts in your life circumstances, financial situation, or external factors.

Incorporate a mix of short-term and intermediate goals within your long-term vision. This not only adds granularity to your financial planning but also provides you with milestones to celebrate along the way. Achieving these smaller goals contributes to your overall sense of accomplishment and motivates you to stay focused on the larger picture.

Lastly, developing long-term financial goals is an iterative process. As you grow, evolve, and experience changes in your life, your goals may also evolve. Embrace the journey of self-discovery, adapting your financial goals to align with your evolving priorities and values.

In the chapters that follow, we'll delve into practical strategies and tools to help you turn your long-term financial goals into a reality. Remember, your financial journey is unique to you, and developing long-term goals is about creating a path that resonates with your dreams and aspirations. As you cultivate confidence in your financial decision-making, envision the life you want to lead and let your long-term goals be the compass guiding you toward a future filled with financial success and fulfillment.

Chapter 3

Chapter 3: Financial Assessment

Welcome to Chapter 3 of "Empowered Finances: A Guide to Financial Freedom for Moms." In this chapter, we embark on a practical and insightful journey – a financial assessment. Think of it as a friendly conversation with your finances, a moment to understand where you stand, identify strengths, and uncover areas for growth.

Just like a health check-up, a financial assessment provides a snapshot of your current financial well-being. It's not about judgment or comparison; rather, it's a tool for empowerment, enabling you to make informed decisions that align with your goals and aspirations.

Consider this chapter as a personal financial wellness session. We'll explore key aspects of your financial landscape – from income and expenses to savings and debts. The goal is not just to crunch numbers but to gain a holistic understanding of your financial picture, fostering a sense of control and confidence.

As moms, we often put the needs of our families first, and our own financial well-being might take a back seat. This chapter encourages you to step into the driver's seat of your financial journey, taking charge with knowledge and intention.

Through the process of financial assessment, you'll gain clarity on where your money is going, identify areas for optimization, and set the stage for strategic decision-making. It's an empowering exercise that lays the foundation for the actionable steps we'll explore in the chapters ahead.

Remember, this is your journey, and there's no one-size-fits-all approach. Whether you're just starting on your financial path or seeking to refine your strategies, the financial assessment is a valuable tool for moms at any stage.

So, grab a cup of coffee, find a comfy spot, and let's dive into the heart of your finances. Together, we'll uncover insights, celebrate achievements, and set the course for a future where your financial goals become not just possibilities but realities. Welcome to the financial assessment – your gateway to a more empowered and informed financial future.

Evaluating Current Financial Situation

Now that we've embarked on our financial assessment journey, let's focus on the first step: evaluating your current financial situation. Consider this as a friendly conversation with your finances, a way to get acquainted with the various aspects of your monetary landscape.

Start by taking a comprehensive look at your income. Identify all sources of income, including your salary, any additional earnings, or passive income streams. Understanding your total income provides a clear foundation for the financial decisions that lie ahead. If your income fluctuates, consider calculating an average over a few months to get a more stable figure.

Next, turn your attention to your expenses. Break them down into categories, such as housing, utilities, groceries, transportation, and entertainment. This detailed overview helps you grasp where your money is going each month. It's not about judgment but gaining awareness. Are there areas where you can optimize spending without sacrificing your quality of life?

Savings are the silent superheroes of financial well-being. Evaluate your current savings – whether in an emergency fund, retirement accounts, or other savings vehicles. Having a financial safety net provides peace of mind and serves as a buffer against unexpected expenses.

On the flip side, let's talk about debts. Identify all outstanding debts, including credit card balances, loans, and any other financial obligations. Understanding the scope of your debts allows you to develop a strategy for managing and reducing them over time.

Consider your investments, if any. This could include retirement accounts, stocks, or other assets. Evaluating your investments involves understanding their performance and ensuring they align with your long-term financial goals. If you're new to investing, this is an opportunity to explore your options and consider seeking advice if needed.

Insurance is often an overlooked aspect of financial well-being. Assess your current insurance coverage – health, life, home, and auto insurance. Ensuring you have adequate coverage protects you and your family from unexpected challenges.

Now, take a moment to reflect on your financial goals. Are they short-term, like saving for a vacation, or more long-term, such as buying a home or funding your child's education? Understanding your financial goals allows you to align your current situation with your future aspirations.

As moms, it's vital to recognize the unique financial challenges and opportunities that may come with the role. Consider factors such as childcare costs, education expenses, and the potential impact of career choices on your overall financial situation.

Remember, this evaluation is not about passing judgment but gaining a clear understanding of your financial landscape. It's the first step toward making informed decisions that align with your goals and aspirations. As we progress through this chapter, we'll explore strategies to optimize your current financial situation and set the stage for a more empowered and intentional financial future. So, take a deep breath, gather your financial documents, and let's continue this friendly conversation with your finances. Together, we'll navigate the intricacies of your current financial situation and pave the way for a future filled with financial success and well-being.

CREATING A BUDGET

Let's dive into a fundamental tool for financial empowerment: creating a budget. Think of a budget as a roadmap for your money, a friendly guide that helps you navigate the twists and turns of your financial journey. It's not about restrictions; it's about aligning your spending with your priorities and aspirations.

Start by looking at your income. Identify your total monthly income, including your salary and any additional sources of income. Knowing how much money you have coming in sets the stage for creating a budget that reflects your financial reality.

Now, let's talk about expenses. Break them down into categories to get a clear picture of where your money is going. Housing, utilities, groceries, transportation, and entertainment are common categories. Be thorough but don't stress about minor expenses at this stage; the goal is to capture the big picture.

Consider fixed and variable expenses. Fixed expenses, like rent or mortgage payments, tend to stay consistent. Variable expenses, such as groceries or dining out, can fluctuate. Understanding these categories helps you prioritize your spending and identify areas where adjustments may be needed.

As a mom, it's essential to include all family-related expenses. This might include childcare costs, school expenses, extracurricular activities, and family outings. Ensuring that your budget accounts for the unique aspects of your family life helps create a more realistic financial plan.

Now, let's turn our attention to savings. Your budget should include a dedicated section for saving money. Whether it's for an emergency fund, future goals, or retirement, allocating a portion of your income to savings ensures that you're building a financial safety net for the future.

Debts are another critical aspect to consider. If you have outstanding debts, allocate a portion of your budget to debt repayment. Tackling debts systematically not only reduces financial stress but also contributes to your long-term financial well-being.

Creating a budget is not about depriving yourself but about making intentional choices. Identify areas where you can cut back without sacrificing your quality of life. It might be finding more affordable alternatives for certain expenses or optimizing spending in discretionary categories.

Consider using budgeting tools or apps to streamline the process. Many user-friendly apps are available to help you track your income and expenses effortlessly. These tools can provide valuable insights into your spending patterns and help you stay on course with your budget.

Remember, a budget is a flexible tool that can evolve with your life. As circumstances change, be open to adjusting your budget accordingly. Life is dynamic, and your budget should adapt to reflect your current needs and aspirations.

Creating a budget is a powerful step toward financial empowerment. It gives you a clear understanding of your financial flow, highlights areas for optimization, and provides a framework for achieving your financial goals. As we navigate through the rest of this chapter, we'll explore additional strategies to enhance your financial well-being. So, grab a cup of coffee, open your financial notebook, and let's continue this journey toward financial success together.

TRACKING EXPENSES

Now that we've delved into the process of creating a budget, let's zoom in on a crucial aspect that adds precision to your financial roadmap: tracking expenses. Think of tracking expenses as putting on a pair of financial glasses – it brings clarity to where your money is going and provides insights into your spending habits.

To begin, let's acknowledge that tracking expenses is not about scrutinizing every penny. Instead, it's a tool for awareness, offering a real-time snapshot of your spending patterns. This awareness is a key ingredient in making informed financial decisions and optimizing your budget for success.

Consider incorporating a method that suits your lifestyle. Whether you prefer the tactile feel of a notebook, the convenience of a spreadsheet, or the efficiency of a budgeting app, choose a method that aligns with your habits. The goal is to make expense tracking a seamless and sustainable part of your routine.

Start by documenting your daily expenses. This might include coffee runs, grocery shopping, transportation costs, or any other expenditures, no matter how small. These seemingly insignificant expenses can add up, and tracking them helps you see the cumulative impact on your budget.

Categorize your expenses to gain deeper insights. Group them into categories such as groceries, dining out, entertainment, and transportation. This categorization allows you to identify spending patterns and pinpoint areas where adjustments may be beneficial.

Regularly review your expenses to stay on top of your financial flow. Set aside time weekly or bi-weekly to reconcile your documented expenses with your budget. This practice not only keeps you informed but also provides an opportunity to reflect on your spending choices.

Be mindful of discretionary spending. While fixed expenses like rent or mortgage payments remain consistent, discretionary spending on non-essential items can vary. Tracking these discretionary expenses helps you make intentional choices and avoid impulsive spending.

As a mom, consider incorporating family-related expenses into your tracking process. Childcare costs, school expenses, and family outings are integral parts of your budget. Ensuring that these expenses are accounted for allows you to create a more accurate financial plan for your family.

Take advantage of technology to simplify the tracking process. Many budgeting apps automatically categorize expenses, provide spending summaries, and even send alerts when you approach budget limits. These tools can streamline the tracking process, making it more convenient and accessible.

Celebrate small victories along the way. Did you manage to spend less in a particular category this month? Acknowledge and celebrate these achievements. Positive reinforcement helps build sustainable habits and keeps you motivated on your financial journey.

Remember that tracking expenses is not a one-time activity but an ongoing process. As life evolves, so do your spending habits and financial goals. By consistently tracking expenses, you remain agile in adapting your budget to align with your current priorities and aspirations.

In the chapters ahead, we'll explore additional strategies to enhance your financial well-being. From optimizing spending to building a robust savings plan, each step contributes to your journey toward financial success. So, keep those financial glasses on, stay curious about your spending patterns, and let's continue navigating the exciting terrain of your financial adventure together.

Analyzing Debt and Credit

Now, let's turn our attention to a critical aspect of your financial assessment – analyzing debt and credit. While debt is a common part of many financial journeys, understanding its impact and managing it effectively is key to financial well-being.

Begin by taking stock of your current debts. This might include credit card balances, student loans, car loans, or any other outstanding obligations. List each debt, noting the total amount owed, the interest rates, and the minimum monthly payments. This comprehensive view provides clarity on the scope of your debt and serves as a foundation for strategic decision-making.

Examine the interest rates on your debts. Higher interest rates can significantly impact the overall cost of your debt. Focus on paying down high-interest debts first, as this can save you money in the long run. If feasible, explore options to negotiate lower interest rates or consider consolidating high-interest debts to streamline payments.

Understand the difference between good and bad debt. Good debt is often associated with investments that have the potential to increase in value over time, such as a mortgage or student loans. Bad debt, on the other hand, typically involves non-appreciating assets or discretionary spending. Analyzing the nature of your debts helps you prioritize repayment based on their impact on your financial well-being.

Assess your credit score and credit report. Your credit score is a numerical representation of your creditworthiness, and your credit report provides a detailed history of your credit usage. A good credit score is essential for obtaining favorable interest rates on loans and credit cards. Regularly reviewing your credit report allows you to identify any inaccuracies or areas for improvement.

Explore strategies for managing and reducing debt. This might involve creating a debt repayment plan, focusing on one debt at a time, or employing debt snowball or avalanche methods. The goal is to develop a systematic approach that aligns with your financial goals and capabilities.

Consider seeking professional advice if needed. If managing debt feels overwhelming, don't hesitate to reach out to financial advisors or credit counseling services. These professionals can provide personalized guidance, helping you navigate the complexities of debt management and develop a plan tailored to your situation.

As a mom, it's crucial to strike a balance between managing debt and meeting family needs. Consider how debt impacts your overall financial well-being and the future financial goals of your family. Prioritize debt repayment in a way that aligns with your family's unique circumstances and aspirations.

Remember that analyzing debt is not about judgment but understanding. By taking a proactive approach to managing debt and credit, you empower yourself to make informed decisions that contribute to your long-term financial success. In the chapters that follow, we'll explore additional strategies to optimize your financial situation and pave the way for a more secure and fulfilling financial future. So, take a deep breath, acknowledge your progress, and let's continue this journey toward financial empowerment together.

STRATEGIES FOR DEBT REPAYMENT

As we delve into the realm of debt repayment, it's important to recognize that managing debt is a journey, and finding the right strategies for your unique situation is key to your financial success. Let's explore some friendly and practical strategies for repaying debt and moving closer to your financial goals.

First and foremost, create a comprehensive list of all your debts. Include details such as the total amount owed, interest rates, and minimum monthly payments. This clear overview allows you to prioritize your debts strategically.

Consider the debt snowball method. This approach involves focusing on paying off the smallest debts first while making minimum payments on larger debts. As you eliminate smaller debts, you gain a sense of accomplishment and motivation to tackle larger ones. It's a psychological boost that can propel you forward in your debt repayment journey.

Alternatively, explore the debt avalanche method. This strategy involves prioritizing debts with the highest interest rates. By tackling high-interest debts first, you minimize the overall cost of your debt over time. While it may take longer to see the tangible results compared to the debt snowball, the debt avalanche can save you money in the long run.

Evaluate your budget to identify areas where you can allocate additional funds to debt repayment. This might involve cutting discretionary spending, negotiating lower bills, or exploring opportunities to increase your income. Every extra dollar you put towards debt accelerates your progress.

Consider debt consolidation as a potential strategy. This involves combining multiple debts into a single loan with a lower interest rate. Debt consolidation simplifies your payments and can reduce the overall interest you pay, making it easier to manage and pay down your debt.

Negotiate with creditors if needed. If you're facing financial challenges, don't hesitate to reach out to your creditors. They may be willing to work with you on a modified payment plan or offer temporary relief. Communication is key in maintaining a positive relationship and finding mutually beneficial solutions.

Explore balance transfer options for high-interest credit card debt. Many credit card companies offer promotional periods with low or zero percent interest on balance transfers. Transferring high-interest balances to a card with a lower interest rate can provide a temporary reprieve and help you make more significant strides in paying down the principal.

Celebrate milestones along the way. Every debt paid off is a victory worth acknowledging. Whether it's paying off a credit card or making the final payment on a loan, take a moment to appreciate your progress. Recognizing these achievements keeps you motivated and reinforces your commitment to debt repayment.

Engage your support network. Share your debt repayment goals with friends or family who can provide encouragement and accountability. Having a support system can make the journey more manageable and less isolating.

Remember, there's no one-size-fits-all approach to debt repayment. Your strategy should align with your financial goals, lifestyle, and capabilities. As you implement these strategies, stay focused on the progress you're making. Debt repayment is a journey, and each step forward brings you closer to financial freedom and empowerment. In the chapters that follow, we'll continue exploring practical tools and insights to enhance your financial well-being. So, take pride in your commitment to debt repayment, stay positive, and let's continue this journey toward a more financially secure and fulfilling future together.

Improving Credit Scores

Now, let's focus on a crucial aspect of your financial assessment — improving credit scores. Your credit score is a numerical representation of your creditworthiness, and it plays a significant role in various financial aspects of your life. A higher credit score opens doors to favorable interest rates, better loan terms, and increased financial opportunities. Let's explore some friendly strategies to enhance and maintain a healthy credit score.

Start by understanding the factors that influence your credit score. Key components include payment history, credit utilization, length of credit history, types of credit in use, and new credit accounts. Recognizing the elements that contribute to your credit score allows you to target specific areas for improvement.

Ensure timely payments on all your credit accounts. Payment history is a significant factor in determining your credit score. Late payments, even if only a few days overdue, can have a negative impact. Set up reminders or automatic payments to help you stay on top of due dates and maintain a positive payment history.

Keep credit card balances in check. Credit utilization, the ratio of your credit card balances to your credit limits, is another crucial factor. Aim to keep your credit utilization below 30%. High credit card balances relative to your credit limit can signal financial stress and negatively impact your credit score.

Avoid opening multiple new credit accounts within a short timeframe. While it's tempting to take advantage of new credit offers, frequent credit inquiries can have a short-term impact on your credit score. Be selective about opening new accounts and consider the potential long-term benefits before applying for additional credit.

Maintain a diverse mix of credit types. Having a variety of credit accounts, such as credit cards, installment loans, and a mortgage, positively influences your credit score. However, don't open new credit accounts solely to improve your credit mix. Focus on a balanced and sustainable approach to credit management.

Regularly check your credit report for accuracy. Errors on your credit report can negatively impact your credit score.

Obtain free annual credit reports from the major credit bureaus and review them for inaccuracies. If you find errors, dispute them promptly to ensure your credit report accurately reflects your financial history.

Consider becoming an authorized user on someone else's credit card account. If you have a trusted family member or friend with a positive credit history, being added as an authorized user on their credit card account can potentially benefit your credit score. Ensure that the primary account holder has responsible credit habits to maximize the positive impact.

Rebuilding credit after financial challenges takes time. If you've faced setbacks such as bankruptcy or missed payments, focus on establishing positive credit habits moving forward. Consistent, responsible financial behavior will gradually contribute to an improved credit score over time.

Seek professional advice if needed. If you're facing challenges in improving your credit score, consider consulting with a credit counselor or financial advisor. These professionals can provide personalized guidance, helping you navigate the complexities of credit improvement and develop a plan tailored to your situation.

Remember, improving your credit score is a gradual process, and there are no quick fixes. Patience and persistence are key. By implementing these strategies and maintaining positive credit habits, you'll contribute to the long-term health of your credit score. In the chapters that follow, we'll continue exploring practical tools and insights to enhance your financial well-being. So, stay focused on your credit goals, celebrate small victories, and let's continue this journey toward a more financially secure and fulfilling future together.

Chapter 4

Chapter 4: Income Optimization

Welcome to Chapter 4 of "Empowered Finances: A Guide to Financial Freedom for Moms." In this chapter, we shift our focus to a pivotal aspect of your financial journey – income optimization. As moms, we wear many hats, and our financial well-being is intricately tied to the resources we have at our disposal. This chapter is designed to help you explore avenues for maximizing your income, whether through your current job, side hustles, or strategic career moves.

Income optimization is not just about chasing more money; it's about aligning your income with your financial goals, values, and lifestyle. As we navigate through this chapter, we'll explore practical strategies to enhance your earning potential and create a more robust financial foundation.

Consider this chapter as a friendly conversation about the various ways you can leverage your skills, experiences, and passions to cultivate a more fulfilling and financially rewarding professional life. We understand the unique challenges that moms often face in balancing work and family responsibilities, and our goal is to provide insights that empower you to make informed decisions about your income.

Whether you're looking to negotiate a salary raise, explore flexible work arrangements, delve into a side hustle, or contemplate a career shift, this chapter is designed to offer practical advice and encouragement. It's about recognizing the value you bring to the table, both in the workplace and beyond, and finding ways to amplify that value in your financial journey.

As we embark on the exploration of income optimization, keep in mind that your journey is unique. The strategies shared in this chapter are adaptable to your individual circumstances, whether you're a full-time working mom, a freelancer, an entrepreneur, or someone contemplating a return to the workforce. We'll cover various aspects of income optimization, providing you with a toolkit to enhance your financial well-being.

So, grab your favorite notebook, find a cozy spot, and let's delve into the world of income optimization. Together, we'll uncover insights, explore opportunities, and empower you to take intentional steps toward a more financially rewarding and fulfilling professional life. Welcome to the journey of maximizing your income and, in turn, maximizing your financial empowerment.

Maximizing Earning Potential

In the pursuit of financial empowerment, one of the key strategies is maximizing your earning potential. Whether you're a mom juggling work and family responsibilities, a professional seeking advancement, or someone exploring new career horizons, understanding how to amplify your income is a pivotal aspect of your financial journey.

Begin by acknowledging your worth in the professional landscape. Recognize the unique skills, experiences, and perspectives you bring to the table. As a mom, you've likely honed exceptional multitasking, organizational, and problem-solving skills – qualities highly valued in the workplace. Embrace and communicate these strengths confidently.

Negotiation is a powerful tool for income optimization. Whether you're negotiating a salary at a new job or seeking a raise in your current position, approach these conversations with preparation and confidence. Research industry standards, highlight your accomplishments, and articulate the value you bring to your role. Remember, negotiation is a two-way street, and finding mutually beneficial outcomes is key.

Consider pursuing professional development opportunities. Upgrading your skills not only enhances your performance but also positions you as a valuable asset within your organization. Attend workshops, earn certifications, or pursue advanced degrees relevant to your field. Continuous learning not only enriches your professional profile but opens doors to higher-paying opportunities.

Explore flexible work arrangements that align with your lifestyle. As a mom, achieving a balance between work and family is often a top priority. Many companies now offer flexible work options, including remote work, flexible hours, or compressed workweeks. Consider discussing these possibilities with your employer to create a work environment that accommodates your unique needs.

Diversify your income streams by exploring side hustles or freelancing opportunities. The gig economy has created various avenues for individuals to leverage their skills and talents outside of traditional employment. Whether it's consulting, freelancing, or launching a small business, diversifying your income can provide an additional financial cushion and expand your overall earning potential.

Cultivate a strong professional network. Networking is not just about collecting business cards; it's about building genuine connections with individuals in your industry. Attend industry events, engage in online communities, and seek mentorship opportunities. A robust professional network can offer insights, mentorship, and potentially lead to new opportunities for career advancement.

Evaluate the potential for career growth within your current organization. Communicate your career goals to your supervisor and inquire about advancement opportunities. Demonstrating your commitment to personal and professional growth can position you for promotions or higher-paying roles within your company.

Consider exploring entrepreneurship or freelancing if you have a passion or skill set that lends itself to self-employment. Starting a small business or offering freelance services allows you to set your own rates and potentially increase your income based on demand for your expertise.

As you embark on the journey of maximizing your earning potential, remember that your professional trajectory is dynamic. Be open to reassessing your goals, adapting to changes in your industry, and exploring new opportunities. The pursuit of maximizing your income is not just about financial gain; it's about aligning your work with your values, goals, and desired lifestyle. In the chapters ahead, we'll delve deeper into specific strategies and considerations for income optimization, providing you with the insights and tools to empower your journey toward a more financially rewarding and fulfilling professional life. So, take a moment to reflect on your professional aspirations, acknowledge your strengths, and let's continue this exploration of maximizing your earning potential together.

PURSUING CAREER ADVANCEMENT

Embarking on the journey of maximizing your earning potential often involves a thoughtful exploration of career advancement opportunities. Whether you're aiming for a higher position in your current organization or contemplating a transition to a new field, strategic career advancement is a powerful strategy in your pursuit of financial empowerment.

Start by conducting a self-assessment of your skills, strengths, and professional goals. Reflect on where you currently stand in your career and where you aspire to be. Understanding your unique value proposition and the direction you want to move in lays the foundation for a targeted and intentional approach to career advancement.

Engage in open and transparent communication with your supervisor or manager. Share your career goals, express your commitment to the success of the organization, and inquire about potential paths for advancement. Establishing a clear line of communication demonstrates initiative and positions you as an invested and proactive team member.

Seek mentorship within your organization or industry. A mentor can provide guidance, share insights from their own experiences, and offer valuable advice on navigating the complexities of career advancement. Establishing mentorship relationships can also broaden your professional network and open doors to new opportunities.

Invest in professional development opportunities to enhance your skills and knowledge. Attend workshops, conferences, or industry-specific training programs that align with your career goals. Continuous learning not only enriches your skill set but also demonstrates to employers your commitment to staying current in your field.

Consider taking on additional responsibilities or projects within your current role. Proactively seeking opportunities to contribute beyond your job description showcases your initiative and dedication. It can also demonstrate to decision-makers within your organization that you are ready for more significant challenges and responsibilities.

Position yourself as a problem solver and a proactive team player. Identify areas within your organization where you can contribute solutions or improvements. By showcasing your ability to add value and drive positive change, you position yourself as an indispensable asset – a quality often recognized in advancement decisions.

Stay informed about industry trends and changes. Being aware of the broader landscape in your field allows you to position yourself as someone who understands the industry's trajectory. It can also provide insights into emerging opportunities for career advancement.

Networking plays a crucial role in career advancement. Attend industry events, join professional organizations, and engage with colleagues both within and outside your organization. Building a strong professional network not only exposes you to potential opportunities but also enhances your visibility within your industry.

Consider seeking out a career coach for personalized guidance. A career coach can help you clarify your goals, identify potential career paths, and develop a strategic plan for advancement. Their expertise can provide valuable insights and support as you navigate the intricacies of your professional journey.

Remember that career advancement is not solely about climbing the corporate ladder; it's about aligning your professional growth with your personal aspirations. Be adaptable to change, open to new challenges, and proactive in seeking opportunities that align with your goals. In the chapters ahead, we'll continue to explore practical strategies and insights to empower your journey toward a more financially rewarding and fulfilling professional life. So, take a moment to envision your career aspirations, acknowledge your capabilities, and let's continue this exploration of career advancement together.

EXPLORING ADDITIONAL INCOME STREAMS

In the pursuit of maximizing your earning potential, it's valuable to explore additional income streams beyond your primary job. Diversifying your sources of income not only provides financial security but also opens up opportunities for growth and flexibility. Whether you're a mom looking to supplement your family income or a professional seeking to boost your overall financial well-being, exploring additional income streams can be a strategic move in your financial journey.

Consider leveraging your skills and passions in the gig economy. The rise of freelancing platforms and gig opportunities allows individuals to offer their services in a flexible and on-demand manner. Whether you're skilled in graphic design, writing, coding, or marketing, freelancing platforms provide a platform to connect with clients seeking your expertise. This can be an excellent way to monetize your skills outside of your regular job.

Explore the possibility of a side hustle. A side hustle is a venture or project that you pursue alongside your full-time job. It can be anything from selling handmade crafts on Etsy to offering consulting services in your area of expertise. A side hustle not only provides an additional income stream but also allows you to explore your entrepreneurial spirit and diversify your professional experiences.

Consider passive income opportunities. Passive income is money earned with little to no effort on your part. This can include income generated from investments, rental properties, or royalties from creative works. While establishing passive income streams may require an initial investment or effort, they can provide a consistent source of income over time, contributing to your overall financial stability.

Explore opportunities for affiliate marketing or partnerships. If you have a blog, social media presence, or a platform where you share information or recommendations, consider partnering with brands or companies through affiliate marketing. This involves earning a commission for promoting products or services. It can be a low-effort way to generate income if you already have an established online presence.

Monetize your hobbies or creative pursuits. If you have a passion for photography, writing, crafting, or any other creative endeavor, explore ways to turn your hobby into a source of income. This can include selling your artwork, writing freelance articles, or offering workshops or classes in your area of expertise.

Consider real estate investments. Real estate can be a significant avenue for generating additional income. Whether it's through rental properties or real estate crowdfunding platforms, investing in real estate can provide a steady stream of passive income over time. It's essential to conduct thorough research and consider your risk tolerance before venturing into real estate investments.

Evaluate opportunities for online courses or digital products. If you have expertise in a particular subject, consider creating and selling online courses or digital products. Platforms like Udemy, Teachable, or Gumroad allow you to reach a global audience and monetize your knowledge. This can be a scalable way to generate income while sharing your skills with others.

As you explore additional income streams, it's crucial to align these opportunities with your skills, interests, and time availability. Finding the right balance between your primary job, family responsibilities, and additional income pursuits is key to a sustainable and fulfilling lifestyle. In the chapters ahead, we'll continue to delve into practical strategies and insights to enhance your financial well-being. So, take a moment to reflect on your skills and passions, consider the possibilities, and let's continue this exploration of additional income streams together.

Budgeting for Single-Income Households

Navigating the financial landscape of a single-income household comes with its unique set of challenges, but with thoughtful budgeting, it's entirely possible to build financial stability and achieve your goals. Whether you're a single mom or someone managing a household on a sole income, this section is designed to provide insights into effective budgeting strategies that align with the dynamics of a single-income household.

Begin by establishing a clear understanding of your financial landscape. Take stock of your monthly income, including your salary and any additional income sources. Identify your fixed expenses, such as rent or mortgage, utilities, insurance, and debt payments. Understanding your baseline financial picture is the foundation for creating a realistic budget.

Prioritize your essential expenses. In a single-income household, it's crucial to distinguish between needs and wants. Ensure that your basic needs, such as housing, utilities, groceries, and healthcare, are covered before allocating funds to discretionary spending. This prioritization helps create a stable financial foundation, especially during times of economic uncertainty.

Create a comprehensive budget that accounts for all your expenses, both fixed and variable. Your budget should encompass not only monthly bills but also irregular or annual expenses. Consider setting aside funds for emergencies and unexpected expenses to build a financial safety net.

When managing a single-income household, it's important to strike a balance between saving and spending. Allocate a portion of your income to savings, even if it's a modest amount. Building an emergency fund provides a buffer for unexpected expenses and contributes to your overall financial security.

Explore opportunities to increase your income. In a single-income household, maximizing your earning potential becomes especially significant. This could involve negotiating a salary raise, pursuing professional development, or exploring side hustles and additional income streams. Every dollar earned beyond your primary income contributes to your financial resilience.

Communicate openly about financial goals and priorities. If you're sharing your household with family members or children, fostering an environment of open communication about finances is essential. Discuss financial goals, establish a shared understanding of budget priorities, and involve everyone in making informed decisions about spending and saving.

Look for ways to optimize your spending without sacrificing quality of life. This might involve exploring discounts, buying generic brands, or finding creative ways to enjoy leisure activities without overspending. Small adjustments in spending habits can add up, contributing to your ability to save and invest in your financial future.

Consider the long-term financial goals of your single-income household. Whether it's homeownership, education expenses, or retirement planning, having a clear vision of your financial objectives allows you to align your budgeting efforts with your broader aspirations. Break down larger goals into manageable steps and create a roadmap for achieving them over time.

Be adaptable in your budgeting approach. Life circumstances can change, and flexibility in your budget allows you to navigate unexpected challenges or seize new opportunities. Regularly review and adjust your budget as needed, ensuring it remains a dynamic tool that reflects your current financial reality.

In a single-income household, every financial decision plays a crucial role in building a secure and fulfilling life. By approaching budgeting with intention, prioritizing essential expenses, and seeking opportunities for both saving and earning, you lay the groundwork for financial stability and future success. In the chapters ahead, we'll continue to explore practical strategies and insights to empower your journey toward financial well-being. So, take a moment to reflect on your financial goals, embrace the process of budgeting, and let's continue this exploration of financial empowerment together.

CREATING A SUSTAINABLE BUDGET

Creating a sustainable budget is not just about crunching numbers; it's about crafting a financial plan that aligns with your lifestyle, values, and long-term goals. In a single-income household, the importance of a sustainable budget is magnified, as it serves as the guiding framework for managing your resources and building financial stability. Let's explore the key principles and strategies for creating a budget that not only meets your immediate needs but also sets the stage for a financially resilient future.

Start by assessing your current spending patterns. Take a close look at your bank statements, receipts, and bills to understand where your money is going. Categorize your expenses into fixed and variable, essential and non-essential. This analysis provides a clear snapshot of your financial habits and forms the basis for building a sustainable budget.

Distinguish between needs and wants. Needs are the essential expenses required for daily living, such as housing, utilities, groceries, and healthcare. Wants encompass discretionary spending on non-essential items or activities. Clearly defining these categories helps prioritize spending and ensures that your budget focuses on meeting essential needs first.

Set realistic and achievable financial goals. Whether it's paying off debt, building an emergency fund, or saving for a specific purpose, establishing clear financial objectives provides direction for your budget. Break down larger goals into smaller, manageable milestones, creating a roadmap that guides your financial decisions.

Allocate a portion of your income to savings and emergency funds. Building a financial safety net is a cornerstone of a sustainable budget. Aim to save at least three to six months' worth of living expenses to cover unforeseen circumstances or disruptions in your income. This buffer provides peace of mind and financial resilience.

Consider adopting the 50/30/20 rule. This budgeting guideline suggests allocating 50% of your income to needs, 30% to wants, and 20% to savings and debt repayment. While these percentages can be adjusted based on your individual circumstances, the principle of prioritizing essential needs, allowing for discretionary spending, and saving for the future remains valuable.

Regularly track and review your budget. A sustainable budget is not a one-time creation but an evolving tool that adapts to your changing circumstances. Periodically review your spending, assess your progress toward financial goals, and make adjustments as needed. This ongoing engagement with your budget ensures its effectiveness in guiding your financial decisions.

Involve your family members in the budgeting process. If you're managing a household with others, collaborative budgeting fosters a shared understanding of financial priorities. Discuss financial goals, solicit input, and ensure that everyone is on board with the budgeting plan. This collaborative approach strengthens the financial well-being of the entire household.

Look for opportunities to reduce expenses without sacrificing quality of life. Sustainable budgeting involves finding a balance between meeting your needs and optimizing your spending. This might include negotiating bills, exploring discounts, or making mindful choices about discretionary spending. Small adjustments can contribute significantly to your financial sustainability.

Celebrate milestones and stay positive. Budgeting is a journey, and achieving financial goals takes time and dedication. Celebrate small victories along the way, whether it's paying off a debt or reaching a savings milestone. Maintaining a positive mindset encourages perseverance and commitment to your financial plan.

Creating a sustainable budget is a dynamic and empowering process. By aligning your spending with your values, setting achievable goals, and regularly reviewing and adjusting your budget, you lay the groundwork for financial well-being. In the chapters ahead, we'll continue to explore practical strategies and insights to enhance your financial journey. So, take a moment to reflect on your financial priorities, embrace the process of budgeting, and let's continue this exploration of financial empowerment together.

EMERGENCY FUND PLANNING

Emergency fund planning is a cornerstone of financial resilience, providing a safety net for unexpected expenses and financial challenges. In the context of a single-income household, where there may be fewer income sources to rely on, having a well-thought-out emergency fund becomes even more crucial. Let's explore the principles and strategies for effective emergency fund planning, ensuring that you're well-prepared for the unexpected twists and turns that life may throw your way.

Understand the purpose of an emergency fund. An emergency fund is a financial cushion designed to cover unforeseen expenses or disruptions in your income. Whether it's a medical emergency, car repairs, or a sudden job loss, having readily accessible funds allows you to navigate these challenges without derailing your overall financial stability.

Determine the size of your emergency fund. The general guideline is to aim for three to six months' worth of living expenses. However, the optimal size of your emergency fund depends on factors such as your income stability, job security, and individual circumstances. Assess your risk tolerance and consider potential scenarios that might impact your income to determine the appropriate size for your emergency fund.

Start small and build gradually. If creating a full six-month emergency fund feels daunting, start with a smaller goal and gradually work your way up. The key is to establish the habit of consistently saving for emergencies. Every dollar you contribute to your emergency fund is a step toward greater financial security.

Automate your savings. Set up automatic transfers to your emergency fund to ensure consistent and disciplined savings. Automating this process streamlines your financial management, making it easier to contribute to your emergency fund regularly. Treat your emergency fund as a non-negotiable expense, prioritizing it alongside other essential bills.

Choose a dedicated account for your emergency fund. Keep your emergency fund separate from your day-to-day spending accounts. This separation helps prevent the temptation to dip into the fund for non-emergencies. Consider using a high-yield savings account, money market account, or other low-risk, easily accessible financial instruments for your emergency fund.

Prioritize replenishing your fund after withdrawals. Life's emergencies may necessitate tapping into your emergency fund. If you do use funds for an unexpected expense, make it a priority to replenish the withdrawn amount as soon as possible. Maintaining the integrity of your emergency fund ensures its availability when needed.

Consider your individual circumstances. If you're managing a single-income household, take into account factors such as job security, the nature of your work, and any potential fluctuations in income. Adjust the size and structure of your emergency fund based on your unique situation to ensure that it provides an adequate financial buffer.

Regularly review and reassess your emergency fund. As circumstances change, periodically revisit your emergency fund size and adjust it accordingly. Factors such as changes in income, family size, or living expenses may necessitate modifications to ensure that your emergency fund remains aligned with your current financial reality.

Remember, your emergency fund is not an investment but a financial safety net. While it may not earn significant interest, its primary purpose is to provide readily available funds in times of need. By thoughtfully planning and consistently contributing to your emergency fund, you're taking proactive steps toward financial security and resilience. In the chapters ahead, we'll continue to explore practical strategies and insights to enhance your financial journey. So, take a moment to reflect on your emergency fund goals, embrace the habit of regular savings, and let's continue this exploration of financial empowerment together.

Chapter 5

Chapter 5: Smart Saving Strategies

Welcome to Chapter 5 of "Empowered Finances: A Guide to Financial Freedom for Moms." In this chapter, we delve into the world of smart saving strategies – an essential component of your journey toward financial empowerment. Saving money is not just about setting funds aside; it's about cultivating habits and adopting strategies that align with your goals, allowing you to build a robust financial foundation.

As we navigate through this chapter, think of saving not as a restrictive measure but as a powerful tool that empowers you to achieve your dreams, handle unforeseen challenges, and create a future filled with financial security. Whether you're a mom managing a household on a single income or someone looking to enhance your saving habits, this chapter is tailored to provide insights and practical strategies for smarter saving.

We'll explore various facets of smart saving, from setting achievable goals and creating a personalized savings plan to leveraging technology and making informed choices about where to stash your savings. Understanding that everyone's financial journey is unique, our goal is to equip you with the tools and knowledge to make saving a seamless and rewarding part of your everyday life.

Saving money isn't just about sacrifice; it's about intentionality and empowerment. It's about aligning your financial decisions with your values, creating a safety net for the unexpected, and gradually building the resources to turn your dreams into reality. So, grab your favorite notepad, find a comfortable spot, and let's embark on the exploration of smart saving strategies together. Whether you're saving for an emergency fund, a dream vacation, or long-term financial goals, this chapter is designed to guide you toward a more secure and fulfilling financial future. Welcome to the world of smart saving, where every dollar saved is a step closer to the life you envision.

Building an Emergency Fund

Building an emergency fund is a financial step that often gets a nod of approval from experts and for good reason – it's your financial safety net, your cushion against life's unexpected curveballs. In this section, we'll explore the ins and outs of building and maintaining a robust emergency fund, understanding that this financial resource plays a pivotal role in your journey toward financial security.

Firstly, let's revisit the purpose of an emergency fund. It's not just a stack of money sitting idly; it's your financial superhero, ready to swoop in when the unexpected happens. Whether it's a medical emergency, sudden car repairs, or a temporary job loss, your emergency fund provides a buffer, allowing you to weather the storm without jeopardizing your overall financial stability.

When it comes to building your emergency fund, consistency is key. Think of it as a gradual process, akin to constructing a sturdy bridge. Every contribution you make is a brick, and over time, these bricks accumulate into a solid structure that can withstand unforeseen challenges. Start small if you must, but make saving for emergencies a non-negotiable part of your financial routine.

Determine a realistic target for your emergency fund. While the standard advice is to aim for three to six months' worth of living expenses, your target may vary based on your unique circumstances. Consider factors such as job stability, the nature of your work, and the number of dependents. Your goal is to create a fund that can cover your essential expenses during a period of financial uncertainty.

Automate your savings to make the process seamless. Set up automatic transfers to your emergency fund each time you receive your paycheck. Automating this ensures that saving becomes a consistent habit rather than a sporadic effort. Treating your emergency fund as a financial priority reinforces its importance in your overall financial plan.

Choose the right account for your emergency fund. Accessibility is crucial here. While you want your funds to earn some interest, the primary consideration is how quickly you can access them in an emergency. High-yield savings accounts, money market accounts, or even a separate savings account with your current bank can be suitable options.

Keep your emergency fund separate from your everyday spending. This separation isn't just about the physical location of your funds; it's a mental boundary. Keeping your emergency fund distinct emphasizes its designated purpose – to be there when you truly need it. Resist the temptation to dip into it for non-emergencies.

Remember that life happens, and your emergency fund is there to help you navigate the unexpected twists and turns. If you do find yourself tapping into it, view it as a lifeline rather than a setback. The key is to replenish it as soon as possible to maintain its efficacy in protecting your financial well-being.

In essence, building an emergency fund is an act of financial self-care. It's about creating a sense of security in the face of uncertainties. As we move forward in this journey, we'll explore additional smart saving strategies, but establishing and nurturing your emergency fund remains a foundational step. Take a moment to reflect on your emergency fund goals, set a plan in motion, and let's continue this exploration of smart saving together.

IMPORTANCE OF EMERGENCY SAVINGS

Understanding the importance of emergency savings is akin to recognizing the value of a reliable safety net. Life is unpredictable, and unforeseen circumstances can arise when we least expect them. In this section, we'll delve into the significance of having a robust emergency fund and why it's a cornerstone of your financial well-being.

First and foremost, your emergency fund provides a financial buffer for unexpected expenses. Whether it's a sudden medical bill, car repairs, or a home-related issue, these unplanned costs can quickly derail your financial stability. Having an emergency fund allows you to address these expenses without resorting to high-interest loans or tapping into your long-term savings, helping you navigate through the unexpected with ease.

Moreover, your emergency fund serves as a lifeline during times of income disruption. In the event of a job loss, unexpected unemployment, or a temporary setback in your income, your emergency savings step in to cover your essential expenses. This financial cushion provides you with the breathing room to search for a new job, pursue alternative income sources, or weather a period of financial uncertainty without sacrificing your basic needs.

The importance of emergency savings extends beyond financial security; it also brings peace of mind. Knowing that you have a designated fund to handle unexpected challenges can alleviate stress and anxiety related to financial uncertainties. This peace of mind is invaluable, contributing to your overall well-being and allowing you to focus on other aspects of your life without the constant worry of financial setbacks.

Building an emergency fund is a proactive step toward breaking the cycle of debt. Without a financial safety net, unexpected expenses often lead individuals to resort to credit cards or loans, accumulating high-interest debt in the process. By having an emergency fund, you create a healthier financial dynamic, reducing the reliance on credit and ensuring that you can address unforeseen expenses without accumulating debt.

Your emergency savings also offer you greater financial flexibility. It allows you to seize opportunities or navigate life changes without being constrained by immediate financial concerns. Whether it's pursuing further education, making a career change, or taking advantage of a time-sensitive opportunity, having an emergency fund provides the financial freedom to make choices that align with your long-term goals.

Consider your emergency fund as a form of self-insurance. While traditional insurance policies cover specific risks, your emergency savings act as a versatile form of self-insurance that can be applied to a variety of unforeseen situations. This flexibility makes it a valuable asset in protecting your financial health across a range of potential challenges.

In essence, the importance of emergency savings lies in its multifaceted role as a protector, a stabilizer, and a source of empowerment in your financial journey. It's not just about accumulating funds for a rainy day; it's about cultivating a mindset of financial resilience and preparedness. As we continue to explore smart saving strategies, keep in mind that your emergency fund is a foundational element, ensuring that you're equipped to face whatever surprises life may bring your way. Take a moment to reflect on the significance of your emergency savings, acknowledge the peace of mind it provides, and let's continue this exploration of financial empowerment together.

SETTING REALISTIC SAVING GOALS

Setting realistic saving goals is like charting a course for your financial journey. It's not just about the destination; it's about the milestones along the way that keep you motivated and focused. In this section, we'll explore the art of setting achievable saving goals – a crucial aspect of smart saving that ensures your efforts are purposeful and sustainable.

To begin, let's acknowledge that saving is not a one-size-fits-all endeavor. Your financial goals are unique to your circumstances, values, and aspirations. Therefore, the first step in setting realistic saving goals is to take a close look at your overall financial landscape. Assess your income, expenses, and any existing financial commitments. Understanding your financial baseline provides a clear starting point for goal setting.

When it comes to saving goals, specificity is key. Rather than a vague target like "save more money," consider defining your goals with precision. Whether it's building an emergency fund, saving for a vacation, or setting aside funds for a major purchase, clearly articulate what you're saving for. This specificity not only helps you stay focused but also allows you to celebrate small victories along the way.

Realistic saving goals are those that align with your current financial capacity. While it's natural to aspire to grand savings achievements, setting goals that are beyond your means can lead to frustration and derail your saving efforts. Assess your income, consider your regular expenses, and determine a reasonable amount that you can comfortably set aside for savings without compromising your essential needs.

Consider the timeframe for your saving goals. Are you saving for a short-term expense, like a home appliance or a weekend getaway, or are you aiming for a long-term goal, such as a down payment on a house or retirement? Understanding the time-frame allows you to establish a realistic saving schedule and adjust your contributions accordingly.

Break down larger goals into manageable milestones. If your ultimate goal is substantial, such as saving for a home, consider breaking it down into smaller, achievable milestones. This not only makes the goal more approachable but also allows you to track your progress and celebrate achievements along the way. Each milestone reached is a step closer to your larger financial aspirations.

Flexibility is a crucial component of realistic saving goals. Life is dynamic, and circumstances may change. Be open to adjusting your goals as needed, whether it's due to unexpected expenses, changes in income, or shifts in your priorities. A flexible approach ensures that your saving goals remain relevant and achievable throughout your financial journey.

Celebrate your successes, no matter how small. Saving is a gradual process, and recognizing your achievements is essential for staying motivated. Whether you've reached a savings milestone, consistently stuck to your saving plan, or navigated unexpected expenses without derailing your goals, take a moment to acknowledge and celebrate your financial victories.

Setting realistic saving goals is a personalized and ongoing process. It involves a combination of self-reflection, financial assessment, and a commitment to gradual progress. By aligning your goals with your current financial reality, defining specific objectives, and remaining flexible in your approach, you create a roadmap that guides your saving efforts toward success. As we continue exploring smart saving strategies, keep in mind that your saving goals are a reflection of your aspirations and a powerful tool in your journey toward financial empowerment. Take a moment to reflect on your saving goals, refine them as needed, and let's continue this exploration of financial well-being together.

Long-term Saving and Investing

Long-term saving and investing are like planting seeds for your financial future – they require patience, care, and the understanding that your efforts today will bear fruit over time. In this section, we'll explore the importance of long-term saving and investing, why they matter, and how they contribute to building lasting financial security.

To begin, let's distinguish between saving and investing. While both involve setting money aside for the future, saving typically implies low-risk, easily accessible funds, often in a savings account. Investing, on the other hand, involves putting money into assets with the expectation of generating returns, which may involve higher risks and potentially higher rewards.

One of the primary reasons long-term saving and investing are crucial is the impact of inflation. Over time, the purchasing power of money tends to decrease due to inflation – the gradual increase in the prices of goods and services. By saving and investing for the long term, you position your money to potentially outpace inflation, preserving and growing your purchasing power over the years.

Investing offers the potential for wealth accumulation through compound returns. Unlike simple interest, which is calculated only on the initial investment, compound returns factor in the accumulated interest on both the principal and previously earned interest. This compounding effect can significantly enhance your returns over an extended period, making long-term investing a powerful wealth-building strategy.

Long-term saving and investing provide the opportunity to benefit from the growth of the financial markets. While short-term fluctuations are normal, historical trends in the stock market, for example, have shown an upward trajectory over the long term. By staying invested through market ups and downs, you position yourself to capture the growth potential of your investments.

Building a retirement nest egg is a key aspect of long-term saving and investing. Contributing regularly to retirement accounts, such as 401(k)s or IRAs, allows you to take advantage of tax benefits while systematically accumulating funds for your post-working years. The earlier you start, the more time your investments have to grow, potentially leading to a more comfortable retirement.

Long-term saving and investing foster financial discipline and a mindset of delayed gratification. In a world that often encourages instant results, the ability to commit to a long-term financial strategy builds resilience and discipline. It teaches you to withstand short-term market fluctuations, resist impulsive financial decisions, and stay focused on your ultimate financial goals.

Diversification is a key principle in long-term investing. By spreading your investments across different asset classes, such as stocks, bonds, and real estate, you mitigate the risk associated with the performance of any single investment. Diversification can enhance the stability of your portfolio and contribute to more consistent long-term returns.

Consider your risk tolerance and investment horizon when developing a long-term saving and investing strategy. Your risk tolerance reflects your comfort level with the ups and downs of the market, while your investment horizon is the length of time you expect to hold your investments. These factors influence the composition of your investment portfolio and help tailor your strategy to your individual circumstances.

In essence, long-term saving and investing are about building a financial legacy. Whether you're saving for a child's education, a home purchase, or your own retirement, the decisions you make today can shape your financial future and leave a lasting impact. By cultivating a mindset of long-term financial stewardship, you position yourself for a future filled with financial security, opportunities, and the ability to pursue your dreams. Take a moment to reflect on your long-term financial goals, consider the role of saving and investing in achieving them, and let's continue this exploration of financial empowerment together.

INTRODUCTION TO INVESTING

Embarking on the journey of investing is like stepping into a world of financial possibilities. It's an exciting and empowering endeavor that can open doors to wealth accumulation and long-term financial growth. In this exploration of investing, we'll lay the foundation with an introduction to the key concepts, benefits, and considerations that make investing a valuable tool in your financial toolkit.

Firstly, let's demystify the concept of investing. At its core, investing involves deploying your money into assets with the expectation of generating returns over time. These assets can range from stocks and bonds to real estate and mutual funds. Unlike saving, where your principal is typically preserved, investing introduces an element of risk and potential reward.

One of the primary benefits of investing is the potential for higher returns compared to traditional savings accounts. While savings accounts offer a safe haven for your money, they often provide minimal interest, which may not outpace inflation. Investing, on the other hand, opens the door to a spectrum of opportunities for capital appreciation and income generation.

Investing also introduces the concept of risk. Different investment vehicles come with varying degrees of risk, and understanding your risk tolerance is a crucial aspect of developing a successful investment strategy. Risk tolerance is a measure of how comfortable you are with the possibility of your investments experiencing fluctuations in value. Factors such as your financial goals, time horizon, and personal comfort with market volatility contribute to determining your risk tolerance.

Diversification is a fundamental principle in investing. Rather than putting all your eggs in one basket, diversification involves spreading your investments across different asset classes and sectors. This strategy aims to reduce the impact of poor performance in any single investment on your overall portfolio. Diversification is a risk management tool that enhances the stability of your investment portfolio.

Time in the market, not timing the market, is a key philosophy in successful investing. Attempting to predict short-term market movements is notoriously challenging, even for seasoned professionals. Instead, the focus in long-term investing is on staying invested through market ups and downs. By holding investments over an extended period, you increase the likelihood of benefiting from the overall growth of the market.

Understanding the power of compounding is crucial for investors. Compounding is the snowball effect that occurs when your investment earnings generate additional earnings over time. The longer your money remains invested, the more significant the compounding effect becomes. This emphasizes the importance of starting to invest early and consistently contributing to your investments over the long term.

Investing is not a one-size-fits-all endeavor. Your investment strategy should align with your financial goals, risk tolerance, and time horizon. Whether you're saving for retirement, a major purchase, or a child's education, tailoring your investments to your unique circumstances ensures that your strategy is both realistic and effective.

In the chapters ahead, we'll delve deeper into specific investment vehicles, strategies, and considerations. Whether you're a novice investor or someone looking to refine their investment approach, our goal is to provide insights and practical guidance to make your investment journey rewarding and empowering. So, take a moment to reflect on your financial goals, consider your appetite for risk, and let's continue this exploration of the fascinating world of investing together.

BUILDING WEALTH FOR THE FUTURE

Building wealth for the future is like constructing a sturdy financial foundation that can withstand the test of time. It involves strategic planning, discipline, and a long-term perspective. In this section, we'll explore the principles and strategies that contribute to building wealth, empowering you to create a financial legacy that extends beyond your immediate needs.

One of the cornerstones of building wealth is consistent and disciplined saving and investing. Regularly contributing to your investment accounts, whether it's a retirement fund, brokerage account, or other investment vehicles, is a fundamental practice. The power of consistent contributions lies in their cumulative impact over time, allowing you to benefit from compounding returns and market growth.

Time is a crucial ally in the wealth-building journey. The earlier you start saving and investing, the more time your money has to grow. This time factor can be a significant advantage, especially when it comes to long-term goals such as retirement. Even modest contributions made in your early working years can potentially result in substantial wealth accumulation due to the compounding effect.

Diversification remains a key strategy for building wealth. By spreading your investments across different asset classes and sectors, you reduce the risk associated with the performance of any single investment. Diversification provides a level of protection against market volatility, contributing to the overall stability and sustainability of your wealth-building efforts.

Understanding and managing risk is an integral part of building wealth. While investments inherently carry some level of risk, it's essential to align your investment strategy with your risk tolerance and financial goals. High-risk investments may offer the potential for higher returns, but they also come with increased volatility. A balanced approach that considers your risk tolerance ensures a more stable wealth-building journey.

Real estate can be a valuable component of building wealth. Whether it's purchasing a home, investment properties, or participating in real estate investment trusts (REITs), real estate can provide both income and potential appreciation. Real estate investments, when chosen wisely, offer diversification and can serve as a tangible asset within your overall wealth portfolio.

Education and continuous learning play a crucial role in building wealth. Staying informed about financial markets, investment strategies, and economic trends empowers you to make informed decisions. Consider seeking advice from financial professionals, reading reputable financial literature, and staying attuned to changes in the financial landscape. Knowledge is a powerful tool in optimizing your wealth-building journey.

Tax efficiency is another aspect to consider in building wealth. Utilizing tax-advantaged accounts, such as 401(k)s or IRAs, can enhance the growth of your investments by deferring taxes on contributions or allowing for tax-free withdrawals in retirement. Understanding the tax implications of your investment decisions ensures that you maximize the efficiency of your wealth-building strategy.

Setting clear financial goals is a guiding principle in building wealth. Whether it's achieving a specific level of retirement savings, funding your children's education, or attaining financial independence, having well-defined goals provides direction and motivation. Regularly reassessing and adjusting your goals as circumstances change ensures that your wealth-building strategy remains aligned with your aspirations.

In essence, building wealth for the future is a dynamic and ongoing process. It involves a combination of disciplined saving, strategic investing, risk management, and continuous learning. As we continue our exploration of financial empowerment, keep in mind that building wealth is not a destination but a journey that evolves with your life stages and financial aspirations. Take a moment to reflect on your wealth-building goals, assess your current strategy, and let's continue this exciting journey toward financial well-being together.

Chapter 6: Navigating Government Assistance Programs

Welcome to Chapter 6 of "Empowered Finances: A Guide to Financial Freedom." In this chapter, we dive into the realm of government assistance programs – a resourceful landscape designed to provide support and relief during challenging times. Navigating these programs can be a crucial aspect of your financial journey, offering a safety net when unexpected circumstances arise.

Life is filled with uncertainties, and there may be moments when you find yourself facing financial challenges that seem insurmountable. Whether it's a sudden job loss, a medical emergency, or other unforeseen circumstances, government assistance programs are designed to lend a helping hand during these times of need.

In this chapter, we'll explore the various government assistance programs available, shedding light on the eligibility criteria, application processes, and the support they can offer. From unemployment benefits to housing assistance and food programs, we aim to provide you with a comprehensive understanding of the resources at your disposal.

Understanding government assistance programs is not just about accessing immediate relief; it's about empowering yourself with knowledge and being proactive in times of need. Many individuals hesitate to explore these programs due to misconceptions or uncertainty about the application process. Our goal is to demystify this aspect of financial assistance, guiding you through the steps to access the support you may be entitled to.

Whether you're a single mom managing a household, an individual navigating a career transition, or someone facing unexpected financial hardships, this chapter is crafted to be a practical guide. We believe that by arming yourself with information about government assistance programs, you enhance your financial resilience and gain the confidence to navigate challenging situations.

So, grab a cup of tea, find a comfortable spot, and let's embark on a journey through the avenues of government assistance together. From understanding the nuances of different programs to learning how they can complement your overall financial strategy, this chapter is designed to equip you with the tools to face uncertainties with confidence. Welcome to the exploration of government assistance programs – a vital aspect of your empowered financial journey.

Understanding Available Assistance Programs

Navigating the landscape of available assistance programs is like having a roadmap during challenging times. In this section, we'll explore the diverse range of government assistance programs designed to offer support in various aspects of life.

Understanding these programs can be instrumental in providing the relief and stability you need when facing unexpected financial challenges.

Let's start with unemployment benefits, a crucial resource for individuals experiencing job loss. Unemployment benefits provide temporary financial assistance to eligible individuals who find themselves without employment through no fault of their own. These benefits aim to bridge the gap between jobs, offering financial support while individuals actively seek new employment opportunities.

Housing assistance programs play a vital role in ensuring stable living conditions for individuals and families facing housing challenges. Whether it's rental assistance, public housing programs, or initiatives addressing homelessness, these programs are designed to provide a safety net for those struggling to meet housing expenses. Understanding the eligibility criteria and application processes for these programs can be essential in times of housing instability.

Food assistance programs, such as the Supplemental Nutrition Assistance Program (SNAP), are geared towards ensuring access to nutritious food for individuals and families with limited financial resources. SNAP benefits are distributed through electronic benefit transfer (EBT) cards and can be used to purchase eligible food items. Exploring the details of these programs can contribute to securing a reliable source of nutrition during financially challenging periods.

Healthcare assistance programs offer relief in the realm of medical expenses. Medicaid, for example, provides health coverage for eligible low-income individuals and families. Understanding the criteria for Medicaid eligibility and how to apply can be crucial, especially when facing unexpected medical costs. Additionally, programs like the Children's Health Insurance Program (CHIP) cater specifically to children in low-income families, ensuring they receive essential healthcare services.

Financial assistance for education is another avenue that can significantly impact individuals seeking to further their education. Programs such as federal student aid, grants, and scholarships are designed to ease the financial burden of educational expenses. Navigating these opportunities requires a comprehensive understanding of the available resources and the application processes involved.

Apart from these key assistance programs, there are various state and local initiatives addressing specific needs within communities. From energy assistance programs to childcare support, exploring the resources available in your locality can provide targeted assistance tailored to your unique circumstances.

Understanding available assistance programs goes beyond awareness; it involves proactive engagement. By familiarizing yourself with the details of these programs, you empower yourself to access the support you may need in times of financial uncertainty. Each program is designed with specific eligibility criteria, application procedures, and benefits. Taking the time to explore these aspects ensures that you are well-informed and can make informed decisions based on your individual needs.

In the chapters ahead, we'll delve deeper into the specifics of each assistance program, providing insights into the application processes, eligibility criteria, and how these programs can complement your overall financial strategy. Remember, these programs exist to provide a helping hand during challenging times, and by understanding them, you position yourself to navigate uncertainties with resilience and confidence. So, let's continue this exploration of available assistance programs, a vital aspect of your empowered financial journey.

WELFARE PROGRAMS AND ELIGIBILITY

Welfare programs constitute a crucial component of the support system designed to assist individuals and families facing financial hardships. Understanding these programs and their eligibility criteria is fundamental to accessing the aid they provide. In this section, we'll explore welfare programs, shedding light on their purpose, the types of assistance they offer, and the factors that determine eligibility.

Welfare programs, often referred to as public assistance or social services, encompass a range of initiatives aimed at providing financial aid and support to individuals and families with limited resources. These programs play a pivotal role in addressing basic needs and promoting economic stability for vulnerable populations.

One of the primary welfare programs is Temporary Assistance for Needy Families (TANF). TANF is a federal assistance program that provides financial support to low-income families with dependent children. The program emphasizes the importance of work and self-sufficiency, aiming to help families transition from dependency to economic independence. Eligibility for TANF is typically determined based on income, family size, and other factors.

Supplemental Security Income (SSI) is another critical welfare program administered by the Social Security Administration. SSI provides financial assistance to elderly, blind, or disabled individuals with limited income and resources. Eligibility for SSI is determined based on factors such as income, disability status, and other financial considerations.

The Supplemental Nutrition Assistance Program (SNAP) is a welfare program specifically focused on addressing food insecurity. Formerly known as food stamps, SNAP provides eligible individuals and families with funds to purchase nutritious food. The eligibility criteria for SNAP take into account factors such as income, household size, and expenses.

Medicaid, a joint federal and state program, offers health coverage to eligible low-income individuals and families. While Medicaid is not exclusively a welfare program, it plays a significant role in providing essential healthcare assistance. Eligibility for Medicaid is determined based on income, household size, and other criteria, and it varies by state.

Understanding the eligibility criteria for welfare programs involves a nuanced assessment of various factors. Income is a primary consideration, with specific income thresholds established for different programs. Household size, expenses, and the presence of dependents are also factors that impact eligibility. Additionally, certain welfare programs may have specific requirements related to age, disability status, or other qualifying conditions.

It's important to note that eligibility for welfare programs is not static. Changes in income, family composition, or other circumstances may affect your eligibility status. Regularly reviewing your situation and staying informed about program requirements ensures that you can access the support you need when faced with financial challenges.

Exploring welfare programs and understanding their eligibility criteria is a proactive step in building financial resilience. These programs are designed to provide temporary assistance during times of need, offering a helping hand to individuals and families working towards greater stability. In the chapters ahead, we'll delve deeper into each welfare program, providing insights into the application processes, benefits, and how they can be integrated into your overall financial strategy. So, let's continue this exploration of welfare programs and eligibility, empowering you to navigate financial uncertainties with knowledge and confidence.

CHILD SUPPORT AND CUSTODY

Child support and custody are integral aspects of family law designed to ensure the well-being of children when parents are no longer in a relationship. In this section, we'll explore the key considerations surrounding child support, custody arrangements, and how these elements contribute to the financial and emotional support of children in separated or divorced families.

Child support is a financial obligation that one parent may be required to pay to the other for the care and upbringing of their child or children. The primary objective of child support is to provide for the child's basic needs, including housing, food, clothing, education, and healthcare. State laws govern child support, and the amount is typically determined based on the income of both parents, the number of children involved, and other relevant factors.

Calculating child support can be a complex process, involving considerations such as each parent's income, the time the child spends with each parent, and any special needs or expenses the child may have. Many states use guidelines or formulas to determine the appropriate amount of child support, aiming to ensure fairness and consistency.

Custody arrangements, on the other hand, determine the legal and physical responsibility of each parent regarding the child. Legal custody refers to the right to make important decisions on behalf of the child, such as those related to education, healthcare, and religious upbringing. Physical custody pertains to where the child lives and how time is divided between each parent.

Custody arrangements can take various forms, depending on the circumstances and the best interests of the child. Joint custody, where both parents share legal and/or physical custody, is a common arrangement that emphasizes the involvement of both parents in the child's life. Sole custody may be awarded to one parent if it is deemed to be in the child's best interest.

Co-parenting is an approach that encourages active involvement and collaboration between separated or divorced parents in raising their child. Effective co-parenting involves communication, cooperation, and a commitment to prioritizing the child's well-being. It often includes creating a parenting plan that outlines each parent's responsibilities, visitation schedules, and how major decisions will be made.

Enforcing child support orders and custody arrangements is crucial for ensuring that the agreed-upon terms are upheld. State agencies and family courts play a role in overseeing and enforcing these agreements, and parents have the option to seek legal assistance if issues arise. Open communication between parents is essential to addressing any concerns and making adjustments to custody or support arrangements when necessary.

Child support and custody arrangements are not only legal obligations but also mechanisms for providing stability and security for children in separated families. They aim to mitigate the potential negative impact of parental separation on children by ensuring financial and emotional support from both parents.

As we navigate through the intricacies of child support and custody, it's important to approach these matters with empathy, understanding, and a focus on the child's well-being. In the following chapters, we'll delve into more specific aspects of family law, providing insights into legal processes, resources, and strategies to navigate these challenges with resilience and care. Let's continue this exploration of family law, acknowledging the importance of fostering positive relationships and support structures for children in separated families.

Making the Most of Support Systems

Making the most of support systems is a cornerstone of navigating financial challenges and uncertainties. In this section, we'll delve into the importance of leveraging available support networks, whether they be friends, family, community resources, or professional guidance. Recognizing that seeking support is not a sign of weakness but a proactive step towards financial empowerment is essential.

Family and friends form the bedrock of many support systems. In times of financial strain, these relationships provide emotional support, understanding, and often tangible assistance. Whether it's a listening ear, childcare assistance, or shared resources, the bonds of family and friends can be a source of comfort and strength.

Community resources play a vital role in extending support beyond personal networks. Local organizations, nonprofits, and government agencies often offer assistance programs designed to address specific needs within a community. These resources can include food banks, housing assistance programs, career counseling services, and more. Exploring what's available in your community ensures you tap into valuable support systems that can augment your financial stability.

Professional guidance is another valuable component of support systems. Financial advisors, career counselors, and legal professionals can offer insights tailored to your specific situation. Seeking professional advice can help you navigate complex financial decisions, plan for the future, and address legal matters with clarity and confidence.

Mental health support is an often-overlooked but crucial aspect of overall well-being. Financial challenges can take a toll on mental health, and seeking assistance from mental health professionals can provide coping mechanisms and strategies to navigate stress and anxiety. Many communities have mental health resources, including counseling services and support groups.

Online communities and forums provide a virtual support system where individuals facing similar challenges can share experiences and advice. Whether you're a single parent, someone navigating a career change, or dealing with debt, connecting with others online can offer a sense of community and valuable insights. However, it's essential to verify the credibility of information and prioritize advice from reputable sources.

Educational resources contribute to building financial literacy and resilience. Understanding personal finance, budgeting, and investment basics empowers individuals to make informed decisions. Many online platforms offer free educational resources, and local community centers or libraries may provide workshops or seminars on financial topics.

Making the most of support systems involves proactive engagement and a willingness to seek assistance when needed. It's a recognition that facing financial challenges doesn't have to be a solitary journey. By tapping into various support networks, you create a web of resources that bolsters your ability to weather uncertainties and make informed decisions.

Remember that reaching out for support is a strength, not a weakness. It's an acknowledgment that everyone encounters challenges, and seeking assistance is a proactive step towards overcoming them. As we continue our exploration of financial empowerment, keep in mind the diverse and valuable support systems available to you. Whether it's seeking advice from friends, accessing community resources, or consulting with professionals, each avenue contributes to your overall resilience and well-being. Let's embrace the support systems around us and navigate the journey to financial empowerment together.

NETWORKING WITH OTHER MOMS

Networking with other moms is a powerful and often underestimated avenue for support, understanding, and shared wisdom. Motherhood comes with its unique set of challenges, and connecting with fellow moms can be a source of comfort and valuable insights. In this section, we'll explore the benefits of networking with other moms and how these connections can contribute to your financial well-being and overall empowerment.

One of the immediate advantages of networking with other moms is the shared experience of navigating the complexities of motherhood. Whether you're a single mom, a working mom, or juggling multiple responsibilities, connecting with other mothers creates a sense of camaraderie. Shared experiences often lead to practical advice, empathy, and a non-judgmental space where you can openly discuss your challenges and victories.

Financial insights and tips are often exchanged within mom networks. Moms may share budgeting strategies, information about cost-effective childcare options, and recommendations for saving money on everyday expenses. This informal exchange of financial wisdom can be a valuable source of practical advice that is grounded in real-life experiences.

Networking with other moms can also lead to potential collaborative opportunities. Moms may share job leads, business ideas, or freelance opportunities within their professional networks. This collaborative spirit extends beyond traditional employment and may include shared ventures, co-parenting support, and resource sharing to alleviate financial burdens.

Childcare solutions often emerge from mom networks. Whether it's arranging playdates, babysitting swaps, or sharing information about affordable and reliable childcare providers, connecting with other moms can offer creative solutions to the often demanding and costly aspects of childcare. These arrangements not only save money but also foster a supportive community where moms can rely on each other.

Emotional support is a cornerstone of networking with other moms. Motherhood brings with it a rollercoaster of emotions, and having a network of understanding and empathetic moms provides a space to share joys and sorrows. The emotional support within these networks can be a crucial foundation for mental well-being, allowing moms to face financial challenges with resilience and a positive mindset.

Professional development and career guidance are often part of mom networks. Moms may share information about job opportunities, offer career advice, and provide insights into flexible work arrangements. Whether you're re-entering the workforce, seeking career advancement, or exploring entrepreneurial ventures, the shared experiences and advice within mom networks can be instrumental in shaping your professional journey.

Social events and community involvement within mom networks contribute to a sense of belonging. Engaging in local mom groups, playdates, or community events not only provides opportunities for socializing but also expands your network of potential resources. From clothing swaps to community resources, these events often reveal hidden gems that can positively impact your family's financial well-being.

In essence, networking with other moms is a multifaceted and dynamic source of support. It goes beyond casual conversations to become a valuable resource for practical advice, emotional support, and collaborative opportunities. As you navigate the financial aspects of motherhood, consider actively participating in mom networks, both online and in your local community. The shared experiences and collective wisdom within these networks can be a guiding force in your journey toward financial empowerment. Let's continue to build connections, share our experiences, and uplift each other as we navigate the beautiful and challenging landscape of motherhood together.

UTILIZING COMMUNITY RESOURCES

Utilizing community resources is akin to discovering a treasure trove of support, services, and opportunities designed to enhance your financial well-being. In this section, we'll explore the vast landscape of community resources available to individuals and families. From financial assistance programs to educational workshops and beyond, these resources form a crucial part of your journey toward financial empowerment.

Local community organizations and nonprofits are often at the forefront of providing valuable resources. These organizations may offer financial assistance programs, food banks, housing support, and career development services. Connecting with these entities allows you to tap into targeted assistance tailored to the specific needs of your community.

Financial literacy workshops and seminars are frequently organized by community centers, libraries, and nonprofits. These educational opportunities cover a range of topics, including budgeting, debt management, and investment basics. Attending these workshops provides valuable insights, equipping you with the knowledge and skills needed to make informed financial decisions.

Job placement and career counseling services are common offerings in many communities. These services can assist with resume building, job searches, and career development. Whether you're re-entering the workforce, exploring a career change, or seeking advancement opportunities, these resources can provide guidance and support.

Housing assistance programs within communities address the critical need for stable housing. These programs may include rental assistance, affordable housing initiatives, and support for those facing homelessness. Connecting with local housing resources ensures that you have access to information and assistance relevant to your specific housing situation.

Food assistance programs, such as community food banks and meal programs, are valuable resources for individuals and families facing food insecurity. These programs aim to ensure that everyone has access to nutritious food, contributing to overall health and well-being. Exploring local food assistance resources can alleviate financial strain related to grocery expenses.

Legal aid services offered by community organizations can be instrumental in addressing legal matters, including family law issues, housing disputes, and debt-related concerns. Legal aid services often cater to individuals with limited financial means, ensuring access to justice and support when navigating legal challenges.

Energy assistance programs provide relief for households struggling with utility bills. These programs, often available through local government agencies or nonprofits, offer financial assistance or discounted rates to help manage energy costs. Exploring these resources can provide relief during times of financial strain.

Educational resources within the community extend beyond financial literacy workshops. Local libraries, community colleges, and adult education programs may offer courses on various subjects, including skills development, vocational training, and entrepreneurship. Accessing these educational opportunities enhances your overall skill set and increases your potential for financial stability.

Connecting with community resources involves active engagement and a willingness to seek assistance when needed. Local government offices, community centers, and online platforms are valuable starting points for discovering available resources. Many communities have dedicated helplines or websites that centralize information about support services.

By utilizing community resources, you not only enhance your financial knowledge and stability but also contribute to the overall well-being of your community. These resources are designed to empower individuals and families, creating a network of support that fosters resilience and self-sufficiency. As you explore the diverse range of community resources available, remember that you are not alone in your journey toward financial empowerment. Let's continue to leverage the collective strength of our communities, tapping into the wealth of resources that contribute to a brighter and more financially secure future for all.

Chapter 7

Chapter 7: Insurance and Protection

Welcome to Chapter 7: Insurance and Protection, a pivotal section that delves into safeguarding your financial well-being and securing a stable future. Just as a sturdy umbrella shields you from the rain, insurance serves as a protective shield for your financial life. In this chapter, we'll explore the world of insurance—unraveling its various facets, understanding its importance, and discovering how it can be a cornerstone of your financial security strategy.

Insurance isn't merely a safety net; it's a proactive measure to mitigate risks and uncertainties that life may throw your way. From health and property to income and life itself, insurance provides a buffer against unexpected challenges, offering peace of mind and financial resilience.

We'll start by unraveling the diverse types of insurance available, each tailored to specific aspects of your life. Health insurance steps onto the stage, ensuring that medical expenses don't become a financial burden during times of illness. Property insurance takes center stage, guarding your home and belongings against unforeseen events. Income protection insurance emerges as a key player, offering support when your ability to earn is compromised.

Life insurance, often a cornerstone of financial planning, will be explored in depth. It goes beyond a mere payout; life insurance is a means of securing your family's financial future and ensuring that your legacy endures.

Understanding the nuances of insurance terms, policy structures, and how to choose the right coverage becomes essential. We'll navigate through the intricacies, empowering you to make informed decisions that align with your unique needs and circumstances.

As we embark on this exploration of insurance and protection, envision it as a journey to fortify your financial castle. It's not just about planning for the expected but preparing for the unexpected, ensuring that you and your loved ones are shielded from financial storms. So, let's step into the world of insurance together, unraveling its mysteries and discovering how it can be a cornerstone in your quest for financial security and peace of mind.

Importance of Insurance for Moms

In the intricate tapestry of life, moms often find themselves at the heart of the family, juggling myriad responsibilities with grace and resilience. In this section, we'll delve into the paramount importance of insurance for moms, recognizing it as a crucial tool in safeguarding not just their own well-being but also the financial stability of their families.

Health insurance takes center stage in the realm of maternal well-being. The journey of motherhood involves numerous medical milestones, from prenatal care and childbirth to postpartum recovery and beyond. Health insurance provides a financial safety net, ensuring that moms can access quality healthcare without the burden of exorbitant medical bills.

Regular check-ups, preventive care, and unexpected health concerns are all part of the motherhood journey, and health insurance is the ally that stands beside moms, offering support during these crucial moments.

Property insurance becomes a cornerstone for moms who are often the custodians of the family home. Whether you're a homeowner or a renter, protecting the physical space where your family lives is paramount. Property insurance steps in to shield against unforeseen events such as natural disasters, accidents, or theft, offering financial support to repair or replace belongings and maintain the stability of your family's living environment.

Income protection insurance emerges as a vital consideration, especially for moms who contribute to the family income. The ability to earn is a valuable asset, and income protection insurance serves as a safety net if unexpected circumstances, such as illness or injury, impede your capacity to work. It ensures that the financial responsibilities of the household can still be met, even during challenging times.

Life insurance, with its profound implications for the future, holds a special place for moms. It goes beyond being a financial tool; it's a gesture of profound love and responsibility. Life insurance provides a financial cushion for your family in the event of your untimely passing, offering support for ongoing expenses, outstanding debts, and future needs such as education or homeownership. It is a poignant testament to a mother's enduring care, ensuring that her legacy of love and support persists.

Navigating the intricacies of insurance terms and policy structures is essential for moms. Understanding the nuances empowers them to make decisions that align with the unique needs of their families. From the deductible in health insurance to the coverage limits in property insurance, knowledge is the key to maximizing the benefits of these protective measures.

In the grand tapestry of motherhood, insurance becomes the invisible thread that weaves through the various roles and responsibilities. It provides moms with the peace of mind that, even in the face of uncertainties, their families are shielded from financial storms. It's a proactive step toward securing a stable future, where the well-being of both moms and their loved ones is safeguarded.

As we continue our exploration of insurance and protection, let's celebrate the resilience of moms and recognize the significance of these financial safeguards in fortifying their pivotal role in the family unit. Together, we'll unravel the complexities of insurance, ensuring that every mom can navigate the journey of motherhood with confidence, knowing that they have a robust financial safety net supporting them every step of the way.

HEALTH INSURANCE OPTIONS

Navigating the landscape of health insurance options is akin to embarking on a journey to secure your well-being and that of your family. In this exploration, we'll delve into the diverse world of health insurance, understanding the options available and empowering you to make informed decisions that align with your unique healthcare needs.

Health insurance serves as a financial safety net, ensuring that the costs of medical care don't become an overwhelming burden. For moms, who often manage not just their own health but that of their entire family, choosing the right health insurance plan is a crucial step in fostering overall well-being.

Employer-sponsored health insurance is a common avenue for many moms. Many companies offer health insurance plans as part of their employee benefits package. These plans often provide comprehensive coverage for medical expenses, including doctor visits, hospital stays, and prescription medications. While the employer typically covers a portion of the premium, employees may contribute to the cost through payroll deductions.

Government-sponsored health insurance programs play a vital role in ensuring access to healthcare for moms and their families. Medicaid, for those with low income, and the Children's Health Insurance Program (CHIP) for children in low to moderate-income families, are examples of government initiatives designed to provide affordable health coverage. Understanding the eligibility criteria and application process for these programs is essential for accessing this valuable support.

Health insurance marketplaces, established under the Affordable Care Act (ACA), offer a platform for individuals and families to explore and purchase health insurance plans. These marketplaces, often operated at the state level, provide a range of options with varying coverage levels and premiums. Moms can use these marketplaces to compare plans, find coverage that suits their family's needs, and potentially qualify for subsidies based on their income.

COBRA (Consolidated Omnibus Budget Reconciliation Act) is a temporary continuation of employer-sponsored health insurance for individuals who experience a qualifying event, such as job loss. While it can be a bridge to maintain health coverage during transitional periods, it's important to note that individuals are responsible for the full premium cost under COBRA, which can be higher than what they paid as employees.

Health Savings Accounts (HSAs) and Flexible Spending Accounts (FSAs) are financial tools that can complement health insurance coverage. HSAs allow individuals to set aside pre-tax dollars for qualified medical expenses, providing a tax-advantaged way to manage healthcare costs. FSAs operate similarly but are employer-sponsored and may have specific rules regarding contribution limits and eligible expenses.

Understanding the specifics of each health insurance option is crucial for making informed decisions. Consider the coverage provided, the network of healthcare providers, out-of-pocket costs such as deductibles and copayments, and any restrictions or limitations within the plan. Additionally, evaluate whether the plan meets the healthcare needs of your family, including coverage for maternity care, pediatric services, and preventive care.

As moms navigate the myriad responsibilities of family life, having the right health insurance coverage is a cornerstone of ensuring the well-being of both themselves and their loved ones. It's a proactive step toward financial security, providing peace of mind that, in times of illness or medical need, the necessary support is in place. As we continue our journey through the landscape of insurance and protection, let's empower every mom to make informed choices that contribute to the health and resilience of their families.

LIFE INSURANCE CONSIDERATIONS

Life insurance is a profound expression of love and responsibility, representing a commitment to the financial well-being of your loved ones even after you're gone. In this exploration of life insurance considerations, we'll unravel the layers of this important financial tool, helping you understand its nuances and guiding you in making decisions that align with the unique needs of your family.

At its core, life insurance provides a financial safety net for your family in the event of your passing. It offers a payout, known as the death benefit, to your beneficiaries, helping them navigate the financial challenges that may arise. For moms, who often play a pivotal role in the family's well-being, life insurance is a means of ensuring that their legacy of care and support endures.

Term life insurance is a popular and straightforward option. It provides coverage for a specified term, typically ranging from 10 to 30 years. If the policyholder passes away during the term, the death benefit is paid out to the beneficiaries. Term life insurance is often chosen for its simplicity and affordability, making it an accessible option for many families.

Permanent life insurance, on the other hand, offers coverage for the entire lifetime of the policyholder. It includes a savings component, known as cash value, which accumulates over time. Permanent life insurance comes in various forms, including whole life and universal life. While these policies tend to have higher premiums than term life insurance, they provide lifelong coverage and the potential for cash value growth.

Determining the right amount of coverage is a crucial aspect of life insurance considerations. The coverage amount, or death benefit, should be sufficient to replace your income and cover outstanding debts, funeral expenses, and future financial needs of your family. Factors such as your income, debts, and the number of dependents play a role in determining the appropriate coverage amount.

Choosing beneficiaries is another critical decision in the life insurance planning process. Beneficiaries are the individuals who will receive the death benefit upon your passing. It's essential to update your beneficiaries as life circumstances change, ensuring that your life insurance proceeds go to the intended recipients.

Understanding the role of riders in life insurance policies adds flexibility to your coverage. Riders are additional provisions that can be added to a life insurance policy to enhance its features. Common riders include accelerated death benefit riders, which allow you to access a portion of the death benefit if diagnosed with a terminal illness, and waiver of premium riders, which may waive premium payments in the event of disability.

Regularly reviewing and updating your life insurance coverage is a responsible practice. Life circumstances evolve, and your life insurance should align with these changes. Whether it's a marriage, the birth of a child, or a change in financial status, staying proactive in adjusting your coverage ensures that your life insurance remains a reliable source of support for your family.

As moms embark on the journey of securing their family's financial future, life insurance stands as a poignant testament to their unwavering commitment. It's a gesture that transcends the tangible, providing a legacy of financial security and love. Let's navigate the realm of life insurance considerations with clarity and purpose, ensuring that every mom can make decisions that resonate with the profound responsibility they bear in nurturing and safeguarding their families.

Legal Protections

Legal protections form an integral part of the comprehensive strategy for safeguarding your family's financial well-being. In this exploration of legal protections, we'll delve into the legal tools and instruments that provide a sturdy framework for addressing various aspects of your family's life and future.

Wills and trusts stand as fundamental components of legal protections. A will is a legal document that outlines your wishes regarding the distribution of your assets and the guardianship of minor children in the event of your passing. It's a vital instrument for ensuring that your intentions are carried out and that your family is provided for according to your wishes. Trusts, on the other hand, offer a more structured approach to asset distribution, providing flexibility and potentially minimizing the impact of estate taxes.

Naming guardians for minor children is a crucial aspect of legal protections, often addressed in a will. This designation ensures that, in the unfortunate event of your passing, individuals of your choosing will step into the role of caring for and raising your children. Choosing guardians is a thoughtful decision that reflects your values and considerations for your children's well-being.

Power of attorney is a legal tool that grants someone the authority to make financial and legal decisions on your behalf if you become unable to do so. This designation is essential for ensuring that your affairs are managed effectively, even in times of incapacity. By appointing a trusted individual as your power of attorney, you provide a safeguard against potential challenges that may arise due to unforeseen circumstances.

Advance healthcare directives, including living wills and healthcare proxies, are legal documents that outline your preferences for medical treatment and appoint someone to make healthcare decisions on your behalf if you're unable to do so. These directives serve as important guides for medical professionals and family members, ensuring that your healthcare choices are respected and followed.

Life insurance beneficiaries and retirement account designations are legal considerations that tie into your overall estate plan. Ensuring that these designations are up-to-date and aligned with your current wishes is crucial. Life insurance proceeds and retirement account distributions are typically not governed by your will, making it essential to keep these beneficiary designations current to reflect changes in family dynamics.

Estate taxes are a consideration in legal protections, especially for individuals with substantial assets. Understanding the implications of estate taxes and exploring strategies to minimize their impact can be integral to preserving the wealth you've worked hard to accumulate. Estate planning, including the use of trusts and other tools, can be tailored to address tax considerations effectively.

Regular reviews and updates to your legal protections are essential. Life is dynamic, and changes in family structure, financial status, or legal regulations may necessitate adjustments to your estate plan. Periodically reviewing your will, trust documents, and beneficiary designations ensures that they remain accurate and aligned with your current intentions.

Legal protections contribute to the comprehensive approach to securing your family's financial future. They provide the legal framework to address various scenarios, from asset distribution to healthcare decisions, offering peace of mind that your wishes will be respected and your family's well-being safeguarded. As we navigate the legal landscape of protections, let's approach it with foresight and care, ensuring that every legal consideration reflects the love and responsibility inherent in nurturing and providing for our families.

CREATING A WILL

Creating a will is a pivotal step in taking control of your financial legacy and ensuring that your wishes are honored after your passing. It's a thoughtful and compassionate gesture that provides clarity and guidance to your loved ones during what can be a challenging time. In this exploration of creating a will, we'll delve into the significance of this legal document and the considerations that go into crafting a will that aligns with your values and intentions.

At its essence, a will is a legal document that outlines how you want your assets to be distributed upon your death. However, its impact extends beyond mere asset allocation. A will is your voice, articulating your desires regarding your estate, the care of dependents, and even the sentimental items that hold special meaning for you and your loved ones.

For moms, creating a will takes on added significance as they often play a central role in the family's well-being. Through a will, you have the opportunity to provide clear guidance on how you wish your children to be cared for in the event of your passing. This includes designating guardians who will step into the important role of raising and nurturing your children with the same love and values you would have provided.

Choosing guardians for your children is a deeply personal decision. It involves considering not only the practical aspects, such as the guardian's ability to provide a stable and loving home, but also aligning their values with yours. A thoughtful selection ensures that your children are cared for in an environment that reflects your beliefs and principles.

In addition to addressing the guardianship of minor children, your will allows you to specify how your assets, including property, investments, and personal belongings, should be distributed. This distribution plan can be as detailed or as broad as you wish, reflecting your priorities and the individual circumstances of your beneficiaries.

One of the advantages of creating a will is the flexibility it offers. You have the autonomy to name specific beneficiaries, allocate specific assets to individuals or organizations, and even include conditions for inheritances. This flexibility ensures that your will is tailored to your unique family dynamics and financial situation.

It's important to keep your will updated as life circumstances change. Births, deaths, marriages, divorces, and changes in financial status can all impact the relevance of your will. Regular reviews and updates ensure that your will accurately reflects your current intentions, providing a reliable guide for your loved ones during times of transition.

While it's possible to create a basic will on your own, seeking legal guidance can be beneficial, especially if your financial situation is complex or if you have unique considerations. An attorney can offer valuable insights, ensuring that your will complies with legal requirements and is crafted in a way that minimizes the potential for disputes among heirs.

Approaching the creation of a will is an act of love and responsibility. It's a way of extending your care beyond your physical presence, leaving behind a legacy that reflects your values and priorities. As we navigate the process of creating a will, let's do so with the understanding that it is a powerful tool for providing comfort, clarity, and support to our loved ones, ensuring that our impact endures in the lives of those we cherish.

UNDERSTANDING LEGAL RIGHTS AND PROTECTIONS

Understanding your legal rights and protections is akin to possessing a compass that guides you through the intricate terrain of legal landscapes. In this exploration of legal rights and protections, we'll unravel the key principles that empower individuals, especially moms, to navigate the complexities of the legal system with confidence and assurance.

Legal rights are the bedrock upon which a just and fair society is built. As a mom, being aware of your legal rights equips you with the knowledge to advocate for yourself and your family. It extends across various realms, from family law to employment rights, ensuring that you are treated fairly and justly in diverse aspects of life.

In the realm of family law, understanding your rights is crucial, particularly when it comes to issues such as custody, visitation, and child support. Familiarizing yourself with the legal framework surrounding divorce, separation, or child custody disputes provides a foundation for making informed decisions that prioritize the well-being of your children.

Employment rights are another significant dimension of legal protections. Moms, who often balance the responsibilities of work and family, should be aware of their rights in the workplace. This includes understanding maternity leave policies, protection against discrimination, and the right to a workplace free from harassment. Knowing your rights ensures that you can assertively navigate workplace challenges while maintaining a healthy work-life balance.

Consumer rights play a role in safeguarding your financial well-being. Whether you're making purchases, signing contracts, or dealing with financial institutions, understanding your rights as a consumer ensures that you're treated fairly and ethically. From protection against fraudulent practices to the right to dispute inaccuracies in credit reports, consumer rights provide a shield against potential abuses.

Legal protections extend to your right to privacy. Understanding the laws that govern privacy, especially in the digital age, empowers you to protect sensitive information about yourself and your family. From online privacy rights to the regulations surrounding the sharing of personal data, being informed ensures that your privacy is respected in various contexts.

Education rights are paramount for moms navigating the challenges of their children's educational journey. Familiarizing yourself with the laws governing education, including special education rights for children with disabilities, ensures that your children receive the support and accommodations they need to thrive academically.

Being aware of your legal rights is only one side of the coin; understanding the avenues for legal recourse and support is equally important. Legal aid services, nonprofits, and community resources often provide valuable assistance for individuals who may not have the financial means to hire private attorneys. These organizations can offer guidance on issues such as family law, housing disputes, and employment matters.

Legal protections are dynamic, evolving to address the changing needs of society. Staying informed about legal developments and participating in advocacy efforts contribute to the collective strengthening of legal rights for everyone. By understanding and actively asserting your legal rights, you not only protect yourself and your family but also contribute to the broader goal of fostering a just and equitable society.

As we navigate the realm of legal rights and protections, let's approach it with a sense of empowerment and resilience. Knowledge of our rights is a potent tool, allowing us to navigate life's challenges with clarity and the assurance that, in the eyes of the law, our rights are not just privileges but fundamental aspects of being treated with dignity and fairness.

Chapter 8: Education Planning for Children

Welcome to Chapter 8, where we embark on a journey to explore the exciting realm of education planning for your children. As parents, nurturing the intellectual growth and academic success of our kids is a cherished responsibility. In this chapter, we'll delve into the strategies and considerations that make education planning a rewarding and proactive endeavor.

Education is a powerful tool, shaping the future of our children and opening doors to a world of possibilities. Whether your little ones are just starting their academic journey or are on the brink of higher education, thoughtful planning can pave the way for a smooth and enriching experience.

As we navigate the landscape of education planning, we'll cover various facets, from understanding early childhood education options to preparing for the costs of college. Each stage of a child's educational journey brings unique opportunities and considerations, and our goal is to equip you with the knowledge and insights to make informed decisions.

Choosing the right educational path involves more than just selecting schools. We'll explore the importance of fostering a positive learning environment at home, engaging with teachers and educators, and understanding the evolving landscape of education in the digital age. Whether you're navigating the intricacies of elementary education or guiding your teenagers through the college admissions process, this chapter is designed to be your companion in the exciting adventure of educational planning.

Financial considerations play a significant role in education planning, and we'll delve into strategies for saving for college, exploring financial aid options, and making wise financial decisions throughout your child's academic journey. With the right planning, you can empower your children to pursue their passions without the burden of overwhelming student loan debt.

Education planning is a dynamic and evolving process, adapting to the changing needs and aspirations of your children. By approaching it with enthusiasm and foresight, you can create an educational roadmap that not only supports academic success but also nurtures a love for learning and exploration.

Join us in Chapter 8 as we navigate the inspiring terrain of education planning for children. Whether you're a seasoned parent or embarking on the adventure of parenthood, this chapter is designed to be a valuable resource, offering insights, tips, and strategies to make the educational journey of your children a fulfilling and enriching experience.

Saving for Education Expenses

Saving for your children's education is a significant and proactive step that sets the stage for their future success. In this section, we'll explore the various aspects of saving for education expenses, providing insights and strategies to help you navigate this important financial undertaking.

The rising costs of education make saving for your children's academic journey more crucial than ever. Whether you're preparing for the expenses of early childhood education, anticipating the costs of elementary and high school, or setting aside funds for college, a thoughtful savings plan is a key component.

Starting early is a mantra often echoed in the realm of education savings, and for good reason. The power of compounding works in your favor when you begin saving sooner rather than later. By starting a dedicated education fund during the early years of your child's life, you give your money more time to grow, potentially easing the financial burden when education expenses come due.

529 savings plans are popular vehicles for education savings. These tax-advantaged plans, sponsored by states, allow you to contribute funds that can grow and be withdrawn tax-free when used for qualified education expenses. The flexibility of 529 plans makes them a versatile choice, applicable to both college and, in some cases, K-12 expenses.

Coverdell Education Savings Accounts (ESAs) are another option worth exploring. Although the contribution limits are lower than those of 529 plans, ESAs offer more investment choices. Like 529 plans, earnings in Coverdell ESAs grow tax-free when used for qualified education expenses.

Uniform Gift to Minors Act (UGMA) and Uniform Transfer to Minors Act (UTMA) accounts are custodial accounts that allow you to save and invest on behalf of a minor. While they don't have the same tax advantages as 529 plans or ESAs, they offer flexibility in terms of how the funds can be used.

In addition to dedicated education savings accounts, consider integrating education planning into your overall financial strategy. Regularly contributing to a general savings or investment account can provide additional flexibility and liquidity. However, keep in mind that the growth in these accounts may be subject to taxes.

Beyond the choice of savings vehicle, the consistency of contributions is a key factor in the success of your education savings plan. Set realistic and achievable savings goals, considering your overall financial situation. Automating contributions can make the process seamless and ensure that you stay on track with your savings objectives.

As your child progresses through different stages of education, periodically reassess and adjust your savings plan. The costs of elementary and high school education may have different considerations than those of college. By staying proactive and adapting your savings strategy, you can align your financial resources with the evolving needs of your child's education.

Engaging with a financial advisor can be a valuable step in creating and optimizing your education savings plan. A professional can provide personalized advice, taking into account your unique financial situation, risk tolerance, and goals. They can help you explore various investment options, assess the tax implications, and make informed decisions that align with your vision for your child's education.

Saving for education expenses is a journey that requires foresight, dedication, and strategic planning. By approaching it with enthusiasm and a commitment to your child's future, you not only provide them with valuable opportunities but also instill the importance of financial responsibility and planning. As you embark on this financial adventure, remember that every contribution is a step toward shaping a brighter tomorrow for your child.

529 PLANS AND OTHER EDUCATION SAVINGS ACCOUNTS

Delving into the world of education savings accounts opens up a spectrum of possibilities, each designed to cater to specific needs and preferences. One standout player in this arena is the 529 plan, accompanied by other noteworthy options like Coverdell Education Savings Accounts (ESAs), Uniform Gift to Minors Act (UGMA) and Uniform Transfer to Minors Act (UTMA) accounts. Let's take a closer look at these educational savings instruments and understand how they can play a pivotal role in securing your child's academic future.

The 529 plan, a star player in the realm of education savings, derives its name from Section 529 of the Internal Revenue Code. This tax-advantaged plan allows you to contribute funds that can grow and be withdrawn tax-free when utilized for qualified education expenses. The flexibility of the 529 plan is a key attraction, covering not only higher education costs but, in many cases, also K-12 expenses. Each state sponsors its own 529 plan, and while contributions are not federally tax-deductible, some states offer state income tax deductions for contributions.

Coverdell Education Savings Accounts, although not as widely known as 529 plans, are equally noteworthy. Formerly known as Education IRAs, Coverdell ESAs offer more flexibility in terms of investment choices compared to 529 plans. Contributions are not tax-deductible, but similar to 529 plans, earnings in Coverdell ESAs grow tax-free when used for qualified education expenses. These expenses include not only higher education costs but also those associated with elementary and secondary education.

UGMA and UTMA accounts, governed by the Uniform Gifts to Minors Act and the Uniform Transfers to Minors Act, respectively, are custodial accounts that allow you to save and invest on behalf of a minor. These accounts are not specifically designed for education savings but are often used for this purpose due to their flexibility. Contributions to UGMA and UTMA accounts are irrevocable gifts, and the assets in these accounts belong to the child. While they don't provide the same tax advantages as 529 plans or Coverdell ESAs, UGMA and UTMA accounts offer greater flexibility in terms of how the funds can be used.

Choosing the most suitable education savings account involves weighing factors such as your financial goals, investment preferences, and the specific needs of your child. 529 plans are lauded for their tax advantages and flexibility, making them a popular choice for many families. Coverdell ESAs offer more investment choices but come with lower contribution limits. UGMA and UTMA accounts, while lacking specific tax advantages for education, provide broader flexibility in terms of how the funds can be used.

Understanding the nuances of each education savings account empowers you to make informed decisions that align with your family's financial goals. It's worth noting that these accounts can be complementary, and some families choose to utilize a combination of them to create a diversified education savings strategy.

As you navigate the landscape of 529 plans, Coverdell ESAs, and custodial accounts, consider consulting with a financial advisor. A professional can offer personalized insights, taking into account your unique financial situation, risk tolerance, and goals. They can guide you in selecting the most suitable combination of education savings vehicles and help you create a plan that aligns with your vision for your child's academic journey.

In the journey of securing your child's educational future, the realm of education savings accounts stands as a dynamic landscape of opportunities. By exploring and understanding the features of 529 plans, Coverdell ESAs, and custodial accounts, you pave the way for a strategic and well-informed approach to financing your child's academic aspirations.

RESEARCHING SCHOLARSHIPS AND GRANTS

Embarking on the journey of education planning involves not only saving for tuition but also exploring avenues to alleviate the financial burden through scholarships and grants. These resources, often considered the unsung heroes of education financing, can significantly contribute to making your child's academic aspirations a reality. In this section, we'll delve into the world of scholarships and grants, understanding their significance and offering insights on how to navigate this realm.

Scholarships and grants are essentially free money for education – funds that do not need to be repaid. They are awarded based on various criteria, including academic achievements, extracurricular involvement, community service, and sometimes financial need. Unlike loans, which accumulate interest and must be repaid, scholarships and grants are a gift that can substantially lighten the financial load associated with education.

One of the primary benefits of scholarships is their diversity. They come in various forms, catering to different needs and demographics. Merit-based scholarships, for instance, reward academic excellence and outstanding achievements in areas such as sports, arts, or leadership. Need-based scholarships, on the other hand, consider the financial circumstances of the student or their family. Understanding the different types of scholarships can help you identify opportunities that align with your child's strengths and circumstances.

Grants, often provided by governmental bodies, educational institutions, or private organizations, serve a similar purpose. They offer financial assistance without the requirement of repayment. Federal Pell Grants and state grants are common examples, assisting students with financial need in pursuing higher education. Additionally, colleges and universities often have their own grant programs to support students with specific characteristics or those pursuing particular fields of study.

Navigating the landscape of scholarships and grants requires a proactive approach. Start by exploring opportunities available at the local, state, and national levels. Many organizations, community groups, and businesses offer scholarships tailored to specific criteria or community affiliations. Schools and colleges often provide information on institutional scholarships and grants available to their students.

Encourage your child to actively seek out scholarship opportunities that align with their interests and achievements. This can involve researching online databases, attending college fairs, and reaching out to school counselors for guidance. Some scholarships are niche-specific, focusing on particular fields of study, hobbies, or even unique personal attributes. By casting a wide net, your child increases the likelihood of finding scholarships that resonate with their individual strengths and aspirations.

It's crucial to emphasize the importance of the application process. Scholarships often require essays, recommendation letters, and documentation of achievements. Encourage your child to put their best foot forward in these applications, showcasing not only their academic prowess but also their unique qualities and contributions.

In addition to local and national scholarships, be sure to explore opportunities offered by colleges and universities directly. Many institutions have generous financial aid programs, including merit-based scholarships and need-based grants. Understanding the financial aid packages offered by prospective colleges can play a significant role in your child's decision-making process.

As you and your child navigate the world of scholarships and grants, remember that perseverance is key. Applying for multiple scholarships and grants may require time and effort, but the potential rewards are well worth it. Scholarships not only contribute to funding education but also provide a sense of accomplishment and recognition for your child's achievements.

In conclusion, scholarships and grants are invaluable tools in the education planning toolbox. They offer financial support, encourage academic excellence, and pave the way for your child to pursue their dreams without the burden of excessive student loan debt. By actively researching and engaging with the multitude of scholarship opportunities available, you can chart a course that not only aligns with your child's educational goals but also opens doors to a brighter and more affordable academic future.

Financial Education for Children

Empowering children with financial education is a profound investment in their future, equipping them with the knowledge and skills to navigate the complexities of personal finance. In this section, we'll explore the importance of financial education for children and offer insights on how to foster a healthy financial mindset from an early age.

Financial education is not just about understanding numbers; it's about cultivating a mindset that promotes financial responsibility, critical thinking, and informed decision-making. Introducing children to basic financial concepts at a young age lays the foundation for a lifetime of sound financial practices.

Start by demystifying the concept of money. For young children, money is often perceived as a magical entity dispensed by parents at will. By introducing the idea that money is earned through work, you instill the notion of effort and reward. Consider involving them in age-appropriate chores or activities, linking their efforts to a small allowance. This early connection between work and compensation forms the basis of understanding the value of money.

As children grow, gradually introduce more advanced financial concepts. Teach them about saving, spending, and sharing. A piggy bank or a simple savings account can be a tangible representation of the concept of saving for future goals. Encourage them to set aside a portion of their allowance or gift money for a special purchase, fostering the habit of delayed gratification.

The notion of spending wisely is equally important. As children express interest in making purchases, involve them in the decision-making process. Discuss the concept of needs versus wants and explore alternatives before making a purchase. This not only teaches them about budgeting but also cultivates critical thinking skills.

Financial literacy also encompasses the understanding of basic economic principles. Introduce the concept of supply and demand, teaching them about the value of resources and the impact of choices on the allocation of those resources. Simple activities, such as setting up a pretend store or organizing a mini-market, can make these concepts engaging and relatable.

As children approach their teenage years, expand their financial education to include more complex topics. Introduce the basics of budgeting, explaining the importance of managing income and expenses. Discuss the concept of credit and debt, emphasizing responsible borrowing and the potential consequences of overspending.

Engaging with real-world scenarios is a powerful way to reinforce financial education. Take advantage of everyday opportunities to discuss financial concepts, whether it's comparing prices at the grocery store, discussing household budgeting, or explaining the basics of investing. These real-life experiences provide practical insights that go beyond theoretical knowledge.

Encouraging entrepreneurial thinking is another facet of financial education. Whether it's starting a small business, organizing a neighborhood event, or creating a simple product to sell, these experiences instill a sense of initiative, resourcefulness, and an understanding of the value of hard work.

Consider leveraging technology to enhance financial education. Numerous apps and online resources are designed to teach children about money management, budgeting, and investing in a fun and interactive way. These tools can complement traditional methods, making financial education both educational and entertaining.

Lastly, lead by example. Children often absorb values and behaviors by observing the actions of those around them. Demonstrating responsible financial habits, such as budgeting, saving, and making informed financial decisions, sets a powerful precedent for your children to follow.

In conclusion, financial education for children is a dynamic and ongoing process that evolves as they grow. By incorporating age-appropriate lessons and experiences, you lay the groundwork for a strong financial foundation. The goal is not just to impart knowledge but to foster a positive financial mindset that empowers children to navigate the financial landscape with confidence, responsibility, and a sense of purpose.

TEACHING KIDS ABOUT MONEY

Teaching kids about money is a journey that spans their formative years, offering opportunities to instill foundational financial principles and nurture a healthy relationship with money. In this exploration, we'll delve into the art of teaching kids about money, emphasizing the importance of age-appropriate lessons and hands-on experiences.

Begin the financial education journey by introducing the concept of money itself. For young children, money can be a mysterious entity that magically appears in the hands of adults. By explaining that money is earned through work, you lay the groundwork for understanding the connection between effort and reward. Engage in age-appropriate conversations about jobs and responsibilities, helping them grasp the fundamental concept that money is a tangible representation of work.

Introduce the concept of savings using relatable tools like a piggy bank. This visual and tactile approach helps children understand the notion of setting aside a portion of their money for future use. Encourage them to save for specific goals, whether it's a favorite toy, a special outing, or a long-term aspiration. This early exposure to saving fosters the habit of setting financial goals and planning for the future.

As children express interest in making purchases, involve them in the decision-making process. When they receive an allowance or gift money, discuss the possibilities of spending, saving, and sharing. This opens the door to conversations about needs versus wants and encourages thoughtful consideration before making a purchase. The act of physically counting money and making choices provides hands-on experience with basic financial transactions.

Introduce the concept of budgeting as children grow older and their financial responsibilities increase. Discuss the idea of dividing money into categories such as saving, spending, and sharing. Help them create a simple budget, allocating funds for different purposes. This not only imparts the skill of budgeting but also emphasizes the importance of balancing financial priorities.

Encourage entrepreneurial thinking by exploring small business ventures or projects. This could involve setting up a lemonade stand, creating handmade crafts to sell, or organizing a neighborhood service. These experiences not only introduce the concept of earning income through initiative and effort but also nurture qualities such as creativity, resourcefulness, and a basic understanding of supply and demand.

Integrate technology into financial education by exploring age-appropriate apps and games that teach money management skills. Many educational apps are designed to make learning about money engaging and interactive. These tools can reinforce lessons on saving, budgeting, and making financial decisions in a digital and entertaining format.

As children enter their teenage years, expand their financial education to include more complex topics such as credit, debt, and investing. Discuss the responsibilities associated with having a bank account, the importance of maintaining good credit, and the potential risks and rewards of investing. Use real-life examples and scenarios to make these concepts relatable.

Ultimately, the key to teaching kids about money is to make the learning process enjoyable and relevant to their lives. Engage them in conversations, answer their questions, and involve them in age-appropriate financial decisions. By gradually building their financial knowledge and skills, you equip them with the tools they need to navigate the complexities of personal finance with confidence and responsibility.

Leading by example is a powerful component of teaching kids about money. Demonstrate responsible financial behaviors, whether it's budgeting, saving, or making informed purchasing decisions. Children often learn by observing the actions of those around them, and your habits become a blueprint for their own financial behaviors.

In summary, teaching kids about money is an ongoing and evolving process that adapts to their developmental stages. By weaving financial lessons into everyday experiences and fostering a positive and open attitude toward money, you provide them with the skills and mindset needed to make informed financial decisions throughout their lives.

INSTILLING FINANCIAL RESPONSIBILITY IN CHILDREN

Instilling financial responsibility in children is a transformative journey that goes beyond teaching the mechanics of money. It involves nurturing a mindset that values thoughtful decision-making, resourcefulness, and a sense of accountability. In this exploration, we'll delve into the art of instilling financial responsibility in children, emphasizing the importance of cultivating positive money habits that will serve them well into adulthood.

One of the fundamental pillars of financial responsibility is teaching children the concept of earning. Encourage age-appropriate chores and tasks that align with their capabilities, linking their efforts to a modest allowance. This connection between work and compensation lays the groundwork for understanding the value of money and fosters a strong work ethic. It also sets the stage for conversations about saving, spending, and thoughtful financial choices.

As children accumulate their earnings, introduce the concept of budgeting. Help them allocate their money into categories such as saving for future goals, spending on immediate wants or needs, and perhaps setting aside a portion for charitable giving. This early exposure to budgeting instills the habit of considering financial priorities and making intentional decisions about money.

Incorporate discussions about needs versus wants as a natural extension of budgeting conversations. When children express desires for toys, gadgets, or treats, use these moments as opportunities to explore the distinction between things they truly need and items they merely want. Encourage them to weigh the importance of their wants against other financial goals, fostering a thoughtful and deliberate approach to spending.

Introduce the concept of delayed gratification by encouraging children to save for larger, more meaningful goals. This could be a special toy, a favorite outing, or even a long-term aspiration like a bike or a gadget. By setting aside a portion of their earnings for these bigger goals, children learn the value of patience, discipline, and the joy of achieving something they've worked towards.

Teaching children about responsible borrowing is another crucial aspect of financial responsibility. As they grow older, they may encounter situations where they need to borrow money, whether from family, friends, or financial institutions. Emphasize the importance of borrowing only what they can afford to repay and the need to fulfill their financial obligations promptly. This lays the groundwork for understanding credit and debt as tools that, when used wisely, can contribute to financial well-being.

Engage children in real-world scenarios that involve financial decision-making. Whether it's accompanying you to the grocery store, discussing household budgeting, or even involving them in planning a family outing, these experiences provide tangible examples of financial choices and consequences. The goal is to demystify the decision-making process and help them understand the impact of various financial actions.

Encourage children to participate in charitable giving as a means of instilling a sense of social responsibility. This not only teaches them about the importance of giving back to the community but also reinforces the notion that money can be a tool for positive impact. Consider involving them in selecting charitable causes or organizations, fostering a sense of agency and empathy.

Lead by example in demonstrating responsible financial behaviors. Children often emulate the habits and attitudes of those around them. By showcasing responsible money management, whether it's creating and sticking to a budget, saving for future goals, or making informed purchasing decisions, you provide a powerful model for them to follow.

In conclusion, instilling financial responsibility in children is a holistic endeavor that involves teaching both the practical and the intangible aspects of money management. By nurturing a mindset that values earning, saving, thoughtful spending, and social responsibility, you equip children with the foundational principles needed for a lifetime of financial well-being. The goal is not just to teach them about money but to cultivate a positive and responsible relationship with it, setting the stage for a future where they navigate financial decisions with confidence and prudence.

Chapter 9

Chapter 9: Building a Support Network

Welcome to Chapter 9: Building a Support Network. In the intricate dance of financial freedom, the importance of a solid support network cannot be overstated. Just like a scaffold supporting a growing structure, a reliable network provides the necessary framework for single moms – and indeed, all moms – to navigate the challenges and triumphs of their financial journey.

Financial freedom is not a solo venture; it's a collaborative effort that thrives on the strength of connections, the wisdom of shared experiences, and the reassurance of knowing you're not alone in your pursuit. In this chapter, we'll explore the significance of building a support network tailored to the unique circumstances and aspirations of mothers.

The journey towards financial independence often comes with its own set of hurdles, and having a support network can be the beacon that guides you through uncertain times. Whether you're seeking advice on budgeting, sharing success stories, or simply finding a sympathetic ear, a supportive community can be a wellspring of inspiration and encouragement.

This chapter delves into the art of forging connections – both online and offline – that resonate with the specific needs of mothers. From local community groups to virtual forums, we'll explore the myriad ways in which you can cultivate relationships that uplift and empower. After all, there's strength in unity, and the stories of fellow moms can be a source of guidance, inspiration, and the occasional dose of humor.

Beyond the camaraderie, we'll also explore practical strategies for building a support network that extends beyond financial advice. From childcare arrangements to collaborative ventures, the network you create can be a multifaceted resource, enriching not only your financial journey but also your personal and professional life.

So, let's embark on this exploration of connection and collaboration. Whether you're a single mom, a working mom, or any mom navigating the financial intricacies of life, Chapter 9 is here to guide you in building a support network that strengthens your resolve, celebrates your victories, and stands resilient in the face of challenges. After all, in the journey toward financial freedom, a network of supportive souls can make all the difference.

Establishing a Financial Support System

Establishing a robust financial support system is a cornerstone in the journey toward financial freedom. In this section, we'll explore the significance of creating a network that not only provides financial guidance but also offers emotional support, understanding, and a sense of solidarity.

Financial challenges are part and parcel of life, and having a support system in place can make all the difference when navigating these complexities. Your financial support system is a network of individuals who understand the nuances of your financial journey, whether it's single motherhood, the unique challenges of parenting, or the intricacies of managing a household on a budget.

The first step in building a financial support system is identifying individuals who can contribute valuable insights and encouragement. This might include friends, family members, colleagues, or fellow parents who have faced similar financial circumstances. Seek out individuals with diverse experiences, as their perspectives can offer a well-rounded view of financial strategies and solutions.

Open and honest communication is key to establishing a strong financial support system. Share your financial goals, challenges, and triumphs with those in your network. Creating a space for transparent discussions allows for the exchange of ideas, advice, and even constructive feedback. By opening up about your financial journey, you not only benefit from the collective wisdom of your support system but also contribute to an environment where everyone feels comfortable sharing their experiences.

Consider joining or forming a financial support group with like-minded individuals. This could be an informal gathering of friends or a more structured group focused on specific financial goals. Sharing the journey with others who are on a similar path can create a sense of camaraderie, motivation, and mutual accountability. It's a space where you can celebrate victories together, learn from shared challenges, and provide encouragement during difficult times.

In addition to personal connections, explore online communities and forums that align with your financial goals. The digital landscape offers a wealth of platforms where individuals share their financial experiences, insights, and advice. Engaging in these communities can provide a virtual support system that extends beyond geographical boundaries, connecting you with a diverse range of perspectives and expertise.

Your financial support system is not only about seeking advice but also about offering support to others. Be open to reciprocating the encouragement and guidance you receive. Contributing your insights and experiences not only strengthens your connections but also reinforces the collaborative spirit of the support system.

Assemble a team of professionals to complement your personal support system. This may include financial advisors, career counselors, or experts in areas relevant to your financial goals. Professionals bring specialized knowledge to the table, offering guidance tailored to your unique circumstances. A well-rounded support system combines personal connections with professional expertise for a comprehensive approach to financial well-being.

In conclusion, establishing a financial support system is a dynamic and ongoing process. It's about cultivating relationships, fostering open communication, and creating a space where everyone can thrive on the collective strength of shared experiences. Your financial support system is not just a safety net for challenging times; it's a vibrant network that propels you toward your financial goals with confidence, resilience, and a shared sense of purpose.

BUILDING RELATIONSHIPS WITH FINANCIAL ADVISORS

Building relationships with financial advisors is a strategic step in fortifying your financial support system. These professionals bring a wealth of expertise to the table, offering tailored guidance that can significantly impact your journey toward financial freedom.

The relationship with a financial advisor is not just about numbers; it's about forging a partnership built on trust, communication, and a shared commitment to your financial well-being. When selecting a financial advisor, look for someone who understands your unique circumstances, values your financial goals, and is genuinely invested in helping you achieve them.

Communication is at the heart of a successful relationship with a financial advisor. Begin by clearly articulating your financial objectives, whether it's saving for your children's education, planning for retirement, or navigating the challenges of single motherhood. The more transparent you are about your goals, concerns, and expectations, the better equipped your advisor will be to tailor their advice to your specific needs.

Regular check-ins with your financial advisor are essential for maintaining a proactive and responsive partnership. These meetings go beyond discussing investment portfolios or financial plans; they provide an opportunity to address any changes in your life, such as job transitions, family developments, or shifts in your financial priorities. The more your advisor knows about your evolving circumstances, the more effectively they can adjust their strategies to align with your goals.

Educate yourself about financial matters to maximize the benefits of your relationship with a financial advisor. While advisors bring valuable expertise to the table, having a foundational understanding of financial principles empowers you to actively participate in the decision-making process. Ask questions, seek clarification on complex topics, and collaborate with your advisor to make informed choices that align with your vision for financial success.

Trust is the bedrock of any effective relationship, and this holds true for your connection with a financial advisor. Take the time to vet potential advisors, considering their credentials, experience, and track record. Personal recommendations and reviews from other clients can also provide valuable insights into an advisor's approach and effectiveness. Establishing trust early in the relationship fosters an environment where open communication and collaboration can flourish.

Recognize that financial advisors are not just there for crisis management; they are valuable allies in helping you seize opportunities for financial growth. Whether it's navigating tax implications, exploring investment opportunities, or adjusting your financial plan based on changing circumstances, your advisor can provide guidance that extends beyond the realm of problem-solving to proactive wealth-building strategies.

Consider the fees associated with financial advice as a crucial aspect of your relationship. Different advisors have varying fee structures, including flat fees, hourly rates, or a percentage of assets under management. Understand these fees and how they align with the services provided. This clarity ensures that you have a transparent understanding of the costs associated with your financial advisor and allows you to assess the value you receive in return.

In conclusion, building a relationship with a financial advisor is an investment in your financial future. It's a partnership that goes beyond the transactional aspects of financial planning, encompassing shared goals, ongoing communication, and a commitment to your long-term success. By actively participating in this relationship, staying informed, and fostering open communication, you leverage the expertise of a financial advisor to navigate the complexities of your financial journey with confidence and purpose.

SEEKING GUIDANCE FROM MENTORS

Seeking guidance from mentors is a powerful avenue for personal and financial growth. Mentors bring a wealth of experience, insights, and wisdom, serving as valuable allies in your journey toward financial independence. In this section, we'll explore the transformative impact of mentorship and how it can contribute to your overall well-being.

A mentor is more than a guide; they are a trusted confidant who provides support, encouragement, and a unique perspective shaped by their own life experiences. When seeking a mentor for financial guidance, look for someone whose values align with yours and who has navigated similar challenges. This could be a seasoned professional, a colleague, a family member, or even a friend who has successfully managed their finances.

Establishing a mentorship relationship is a two-way street. While you benefit from the mentor's experience, your mentor gains fulfillment from sharing their knowledge and contributing to your growth. Approach mentorship as a collaborative journey where both parties learn from each other, fostering a dynamic and reciprocal relationship.

Effective communication is essential in mentorship. Clearly articulate your financial goals, challenges, and aspirations to your mentor. This transparency not only allows your mentor to provide targeted advice but also deepens the connection, creating an environment where open dialogue thrives. Don't be afraid to ask questions and seek clarification on financial concepts; a good mentor is not just a source of answers but a guide who empowers you to make informed decisions.

Mentors can provide valuable insights into career development, financial planning, and even work-life balance. Beyond the financial realm, they can share strategies for personal growth, time management, and navigating the complexities of single motherhood. Engaging in conversations that extend beyond finances allows you to benefit from their holistic perspective, enriching both your personal and financial life.

Look for mentors who challenge you to think beyond your current circumstances and envision a future of possibilities. A mentor should inspire you to set ambitious financial goals, offering guidance on the steps to achieve them. Their encouragement serves as a motivational force, instilling confidence and a belief in your ability to overcome obstacles and reach new heights.

Consider joining mentorship programs or organizations that connect individuals seeking guidance with experienced mentors. These structured programs often provide a framework for mentorship, offering resources, networking opportunities, and a platform to connect with mentors who have a genuine interest in fostering personal and financial growth.

Be receptive to feedback and constructive criticism from your mentor. This input is a valuable component of your growth journey, offering perspectives that may not be immediately apparent. Embrace the opportunity to learn from your mentor's experiences, both successes and setbacks, and apply these lessons to your own financial decisions.

Recognize that mentorship is not a one-size-fits-all approach. You may benefit from having multiple mentors who specialize in different aspects of your life, such as career development, financial planning, or personal well-being. Each mentor contributes a unique perspective, enhancing your overall support network.

In conclusion, seeking guidance from mentors is a dynamic and enriching process that goes beyond financial advice. It's about building meaningful connections with individuals who have walked a similar path and are eager to share their insights. By embracing mentorship, you tap into a wellspring of knowledge, inspiration, and encouragement that propels you toward your financial goals and beyond.

Emotional Support for Financial Wellness

Emotional support is a cornerstone of holistic financial wellness, playing a pivotal role in navigating the twists and turns of your financial journey. In this section, we'll delve into the significance of emotional support, how it contributes to your overall well-being, and strategies for cultivating a support system that nurtures both your financial and emotional health.

Financial challenges can elicit a range of emotions – from stress and anxiety to feelings of uncertainty and overwhelm. Recognizing the emotional impact of financial decisions is a crucial step toward achieving a balanced and sustainable financial life. Emotional support provides a cushion during times of difficulty, offering understanding, empathy, and a safe space to express your feelings.

Family and friends often form the bedrock of emotional support. Share your financial concerns, victories, and progress with those close to you. These individuals can provide a listening ear, offer words of encouragement, and celebrate your successes, creating a sense of shared purpose in your financial journey. When challenges arise, their support becomes a source of strength, helping you face adversity with resilience.

Consider joining support groups or communities that focus on both financial and emotional well-being. These groups provide a platform to connect with individuals who are navigating similar challenges. Sharing experiences, challenges, and coping strategies fosters a sense of camaraderie, reminding you that you're not alone in your journey. Whether in-person or online, these communities offer a space where you can be heard, understood, and supported.

Professional counselors or therapists specializing in financial therapy can be valuable allies in your emotional well-being. Financial therapy explores the intersection of emotions and money, helping you understand and address the underlying feelings that may impact your financial decisions. Working with a professional provides a confidential and judgment-free environment where you can explore your relationship with money and develop coping mechanisms for emotional challenges.

Self-reflection is a powerful tool for emotional well-being. Take time to assess your emotional responses to financial situations, identify triggers, and explore healthy ways to cope.

This introspective journey allows you to develop emotional resilience, empowering you to face financial challenges with a balanced mindset and a greater sense of control.

Incorporate stress-relief activities into your routine to nurture both your mental and emotional health. Whether it's practicing mindfulness, engaging in physical exercise, or pursuing hobbies that bring you joy, these activities contribute to a positive emotional state. As you cultivate emotional well-being, you're better equipped to approach financial decisions with a clear mind and a sense of calm.

Recognize the importance of setting realistic expectations for yourself. Financial journeys have ups and downs, and acknowledging that setbacks are a natural part of the process helps you approach challenges with a healthier perspective. Give yourself permission to celebrate small victories and learn from experiences, fostering a mindset of continuous growth.

Communication is a linchpin in emotional support. Engage in open and honest conversations with those in your support system. Share not only your financial goals but also your emotional needs. Clearly expressing your feelings and seeking support when necessary strengthens your connections and reinforces the understanding that emotional well-being is an integral aspect of financial wellness.

In conclusion, emotional support is the invisible hand that guides you through the peaks and valleys of your financial journey. By nurturing connections with family, friends, support groups, and professionals, you create a robust support system that acknowledges the emotional dimensions of financial decisions. As you prioritize emotional well-being, you pave the way for a balanced and sustainable approach to financial wellness, where your resilience and strength shine through even in the face of challenges.

COMMUNICATING WITH FAMILY AND FRIENDS

Communicating with family and friends about your financial journey is a crucial aspect of building a robust support system. These individuals play an integral role in your life, and sharing your financial experiences with them can strengthen your connections and provide valuable emotional support.

When opening up about your financial situation, choose a setting that allows for focused and comfortable conversation. This might be during a casual gathering, a one-on-one discussion, or even a virtual chat. Creating an environment where everyone feels at ease promotes honest and open communication.

Clearly articulate your financial goals, challenges, and the steps you're taking to achieve them. Transparency lays the foundation for understanding and empathy. Share not only the victories but also the obstacles you're facing. This authenticity invites your loved ones into your financial journey, fostering a sense of shared responsibility and collaboration.

Educate your family and friends about financial matters that are important to you. This might include your approach to budgeting, saving, investing, or any financial goals you're actively pursuing. Providing context helps them understand the rationale behind your financial decisions and enables more meaningful conversations about shared values and priorities.

Be receptive to questions and concerns from your family and friends. They may have insights, experiences, or perspectives that you haven't considered. Encourage an open dialogue where everyone feels comfortable expressing their thoughts. This two-way communication enriches the conversation, allowing for a more comprehensive understanding of each other's viewpoints.

Acknowledge the emotional aspects of financial discussions. Money is often tied to emotions, and conversations about finances can evoke a range of feelings. Be mindful of the emotional nuances and create a space where everyone feels heard and validated. This emotional connection strengthens the bonds within your support system.

Celebrate your financial victories together. Whether it's reaching a savings milestone, successfully paying off debt, or achieving a career-related goal, share these moments of triumph with your family and friends. Celebrating together creates a positive atmosphere, reinforcing the sense of shared success and encouraging ongoing support.

In times of financial challenge, be honest about your needs and concerns. Your family and friends are there to support you, and being transparent about your struggles allows them to offer the emotional support you may need. Vulnerability fosters deeper connections and reinforces the understanding that everyone faces financial challenges at different points in their lives.

Encourage financial literacy within your circle. If you've acquired knowledge about managing finances, share it with your family and friends. This might involve discussing budgeting techniques, investment strategies, or tips for improving financial habits. By fostering financial literacy, you empower your loved ones to make informed decisions and contribute to a supportive financial community.

Understand that everyone has their unique financial situation, and comparisons may not always be helpful. While sharing experiences and advice is valuable, avoid creating an environment where individuals feel pressured or judged based on their financial choices. Emphasize mutual understanding and encouragement rather than comparison.

In conclusion, communicating with family and friends about your financial journey is a vital step in building a strong support system. By fostering open and transparent discussions, you create a foundation of understanding, empathy, and shared values. As you navigate the complexities of your financial life together, this support system becomes a source of strength, encouragement, and resilience.

JOINING SUPPORTIVE COMMUNITIES

Joining supportive communities dedicated to both financial and emotional well-being can be a transformative step in your journey toward financial freedom. These communities offer a space where individuals facing similar challenges come together to share experiences, provide encouragement, and foster a sense of belonging.

One of the key benefits of joining a supportive community is the opportunity to connect with people who understand the intricacies of your financial journey. Whether you're a single mom, a professional navigating career transitions, or someone seeking to overcome debt, these communities bring together individuals with diverse backgrounds but shared goals. This diversity creates an environment where you can learn from a range of experiences and perspectives.

Online platforms and forums dedicated to personal finance and well-being provide accessible and inclusive spaces for individuals seeking support. Participating in discussions, sharing your own experiences, and learning from the experiences of others contribute to a sense of community. Engaging with these online communities allows you to connect with people from various walks of life, breaking down geographical barriers and providing a diverse range of insights.

Supportive communities often host events, webinars, or workshops focused on financial education and emotional well-being. These events offer opportunities to deepen your knowledge, learn new strategies, and connect with experts in the field. By actively participating in these educational initiatives, you not only enhance your financial literacy but also contribute to the collaborative learning environment within the community.

Shared values form the foundation of supportive communities. Whether the community is centered around frugality, debt reduction, or financial independence, the alignment of values creates a sense of camaraderie. This shared sense of purpose fosters a community spirit where individuals celebrate each other's successes, provide encouragement during challenges, and share valuable resources and tips.

Supportive communities offer a safe space for expressing vulnerability. Whether you're celebrating a financial milestone or facing a setback, these communities provide a non-judgmental environment where individuals can openly share their experiences and emotions. This vulnerability creates authentic connections and reinforces the understanding that everyone, regardless of their financial situation, is on a unique and evolving journey.

Networking within supportive communities can lead to meaningful connections and opportunities. Whether it's forming mentorship relationships, collaborating on projects, or discovering new career prospects, the connections made within these communities extend beyond the digital realm. Actively engaging with fellow community members opens doors to a network of individuals who are not only supportive but also potential collaborators in various aspects of your life.

Supportive communities often emphasize the importance of self-care and well-being alongside financial discussions. This holistic approach recognizes that emotional and mental health are integral components of overall wellness. Engaging in conversations about stress management, work-life balance, and mental health initiatives within these communities reinforces the understanding that a balanced life involves more than just financial success.

Contributing to the community is a fulfilling aspect of participation. As you gain insights and experiences, you can pay it forward by offering guidance to those who are earlier in their journey. Becoming an active member within the community not only strengthens your connection with others but also allows you to make a positive impact on the lives of those seeking support.

In conclusion, joining supportive communities dedicated to financial and emotional well-being enriches your journey toward financial freedom. These communities provide a space where individuals connect, learn, and support each other in a collaborative and non-judgmental environment. By actively participating in these communities, you not only enhance your own well-being but also contribute to the collective strength and resilience of the community as a whole.

Chapter 10: Entrepreneurship and Side Hustles

Welcome to Chapter 10: Entrepreneurship and Side Hustles, a dynamic exploration into the world of creating your own opportunities and carving out additional streams of income. In this chapter, we'll delve into the empowering realm of entrepreneurship, uncovering the potential of side hustles, and providing insights to help you navigate the exciting path of building your own business.

Embarking on the journey of entrepreneurship and cultivating side hustles isn't just about financial gain; it's a profound expression of your skills, passions, and the unique value you bring to the world. Whether you're considering launching a small business, freelancing, or exploring creative outlets that can generate income, this chapter is designed to inspire and guide you.

We'll explore the mindset needed to thrive as an entrepreneur, understanding the landscape of side hustles, and practical steps to kickstart your venture. Entrepreneurship is a journey that demands resilience, creativity, and adaptability, and we're here to equip you with the tools and insights to make your entrepreneurial dreams a reality.

Throughout this chapter, you'll discover stories of individuals who turned their passions into thriving businesses and learn from their experiences. We'll discuss the importance of identifying opportunities, creating a sustainable business model, and balancing the demands of entrepreneurship with other aspects of your life.

Whether you're seeking financial independence, pursuing a passion project, or looking for a flexible way to generate income, the world of entrepreneurship and side hustles is brimming with possibilities. As we dive into this chapter, consider it your guide to unlocking the door to new opportunities, embracing your entrepreneurial spirit, and charting a course toward financial success and personal fulfillment. Get ready to explore, learn, and unleash your potential in the vibrant landscape of entrepreneurship and side hustles.

Exploring Entrepreneurial Opportunities

Embarking on the journey of entrepreneurship is a thrilling venture that invites you to explore and identify opportunities where your passion and skills intersect with market demand. In this section, we'll delve into the art of exploring entrepreneurial opportunities, helping you navigate the landscape, uncover hidden potentials, and set the stage for a successful venture.

The first step in exploring entrepreneurial opportunities is to take a close look at your passions and interests. What activities make you come alive? What skills do you possess that can be leveraged to create value? Consider the intersection of your talents, interests, and what the market needs. This sweet spot is where entrepreneurial magic often happens.

Market research becomes your compass as you embark on the exploration phase. Investigate current trends, identify gaps in the market, and understand the needs and desires of your potential customers. This research not only provides valuable insights into your chosen industry but also helps you position your venture strategically.

Networking and connecting with like-minded individuals can open doors to unexpected opportunities. Attend industry events, join online communities, and engage in conversations with entrepreneurs in your field of interest. These interactions not only broaden your perspective but also present opportunities for collaboration and mentorship.

Consider the power of innovation in identifying entrepreneurial opportunities. What unique solutions can you bring to the table? How can you differentiate yourself in a crowded market? Innovation doesn't always mean creating something entirely new; it can also involve improving existing products or services in a way that meets the evolving needs of consumers.

Entrepreneurial opportunities often emerge from solving problems. Identify pain points in your own life or observe challenges faced by others. Creating solutions to these problems can form the foundation of a viable business. The best businesses often address real-world challenges and provide practical solutions.

Flexibility and adaptability are key attributes when exploring entrepreneurial opportunities. The business landscape is dynamic, and being open to adjusting your approach based on feedback and market shifts is crucial. Stay attuned to changes in consumer behavior, technology, and industry trends, and be willing to pivot when necessary.

Exploring entrepreneurial opportunities also involves assessing the feasibility and viability of your ideas. Conduct a detailed analysis of the costs involved, potential revenue streams, and the overall sustainability of your venture. This process helps you make informed decisions and ensures that your entrepreneurial journey is built on a solid foundation.

Don't be afraid to start small and test your ideas before fully committing. Launching a pilot version of your product or service allows you to gather feedback, refine your offering, and build momentum gradually. This iterative process is a natural part of entrepreneurship and sets the stage for continuous improvement.

In conclusion, exploring entrepreneurial opportunities is a dynamic and creative process that involves aligning your passions, conducting thorough research, and staying open to innovation. By understanding market dynamics, connecting with others in your industry, and solving real-world problems, you can uncover the entrepreneurial opportunities that align with your vision and potential. As you embark on this exploration, remember that each step forward is a valuable learning experience that brings you closer to building a successful and fulfilling venture.

IDENTIFYING MARKETABLE SKILLS

Identifying marketable skills is a pivotal aspect of your entrepreneurial journey, as it forms the bedrock upon which you'll build your venture. In this section, we'll explore the process of recognizing and leveraging your skills to create value in the market, ultimately contributing to the success of your entrepreneurial endeavors.

Begin by taking an inventory of your skills, both hard and soft. Hard skills refer to the specific technical abilities and knowledge you've acquired, while soft skills encompass your interpersonal and emotional intelligence. This comprehensive understanding of your skill set serves as the foundation for determining how you can contribute to the market.

Consider the skills you genuinely enjoy utilizing. Passion and enthusiasm can be powerful motivators that drive your entrepreneurial pursuits. When you align your skills with your genuine interests, your work becomes more than just a job – it becomes a fulfilling expression of your abilities and passion.

Evaluate the market demand for your skills. Conduct research to identify industries or niches where your particular expertise is sought after. By understanding the demand for your skills, you position yourself strategically, ensuring that your entrepreneurial venture addresses a genuine need in the market.

Embrace the concept of versatility. While specialization is valuable, having a diverse skill set can open up a myriad of entrepreneurial opportunities. Assess how your skills can be applied across different contexts or industries, providing flexibility and adaptability in the dynamic landscape of entrepreneurship.

Look for transferable skills that can be applied in various settings. These are skills that transcend specific industries and can be valuable assets in different business environments. For example, communication, problem-solving, and project management skills are often transferable and highly sought after by employers and clients alike.

Recognize the potential for skill development and enhancement. The entrepreneurial journey is a continuous learning experience, and being open to acquiring new skills expands your toolkit. Identify areas where you can upskill or acquire complementary skills that enhance the value you bring to the market.

Seek feedback from mentors, peers, or industry professionals. External perspectives can provide valuable insights into the strengths and unique aspects of your skill set that you might overlook. Constructive feedback not only validates your existing skills but can also highlight areas for improvement or refinement.

Consider how your skills align with emerging trends and technological advancements. The entrepreneurial landscape is continually evolving, and staying ahead of the curve involves adapting your skills to meet the changing demands of the market. Stay informed about industry trends and explore how your skills can remain relevant in a dynamic business environment.

Explore collaboration opportunities where your skills complement those of others. Entrepreneurship doesn't have to be a solitary journey. Partnering with individuals who possess skills that complement your own can lead to innovative solutions and the creation of a more robust and well-rounded business.

In conclusion, identifying marketable skills is a multifaceted process that involves self-reflection, market research, and a commitment to continuous learning. By recognizing the value of your skills, aligning them with market demands, and staying open to growth and collaboration, you position yourself for success in the entrepreneurial landscape. Your skills are not just assets; they are the building blocks that enable you to create, innovate, and contribute meaningfully to the world of entrepreneurship.

STARTING A SMALL BUSINESS

Embarking on the journey of starting a small business is an exhilarating venture that allows you to turn your entrepreneurial dreams into reality. In this section, we'll explore the essential aspects of launching your own business, from conceptualizing your idea to navigating the initial steps of establishing a small and thriving enterprise.

Begin by crystallizing your business idea. What problem does your business solve, and how does it meet the needs of your target audience? Clarifying your value proposition is essential in articulating the unique selling points that will set your small business apart in the market. Your idea is the seed from which your entire business will grow, so take the time to nurture and refine it.

Conduct thorough market research to gain insights into your industry, target market, and competitors. Understanding the competitive landscape helps you identify opportunities, anticipate challenges, and refine your business model. Market research serves as a compass, guiding your decisions and ensuring that your small business is positioned strategically within the market.

Create a comprehensive business plan that outlines your business goals, target audience, marketing strategy, financial projections, and operational plan. A well-crafted business plan not only serves as a roadmap for your entrepreneurial journey but also becomes a valuable tool when seeking funding, partnerships, or support. It forces you to think critically about every aspect of your business and articulate your vision in a structured manner.

Navigate the legalities of starting a small business by registering your business name, obtaining the necessary licenses, and complying with local regulations. Each region has specific requirements for business registration and compliance, so familiarize yourself with the legal landscape to ensure a smooth and lawful start to your entrepreneurial venture.

Build a strong online presence for your small business. In today's digital age, having a professional website and leveraging social media platforms are integral to reaching your target audience. Establishing an online presence not only enhances your visibility but also provides a platform for engaging with potential customers and building brand awareness.

Cultivate a network of support. Starting a small business can be a challenging endeavor, and having a support system can provide valuable guidance, encouragement, and practical insights. Connect with other entrepreneurs, join industry-specific groups, and seek out mentors who can share their experiences and wisdom.

Secure funding for your small business. Whether through personal savings, loans, investors, or crowdfunding, having the necessary capital is vital for launching and sustaining your venture. Evaluate your financial needs realistically and explore the various funding options available to entrepreneurs, aligning them with your business model and growth strategy.

Prioritize customer satisfaction and feedback. Building strong relationships with your customers fosters loyalty and word-of-mouth marketing. Actively seek feedback, listen to your customers' needs, and continuously refine your products or services based on their input. A satisfied customer not only becomes a repeat customer but also a brand ambassador who can attract new business.

Stay adaptable and open to iteration. The entrepreneurial journey is a dynamic process that requires flexibility and a willingness to adapt to changing circumstances. Be open to learning from both successes and setbacks, iterate on your strategies, and embrace the evolving nature of your small business.

In conclusion, starting a small business is a rewarding and challenging undertaking that requires careful planning, dedication, and resilience. By conceptualizing a solid business idea, conducting thorough research, navigating legal requirements, building an online presence, securing funding, prioritizing customer satisfaction, and staying adaptable, you set the stage for a successful entrepreneurial venture. Remember that the journey of entrepreneurship is as much about the process as it is about the destination, and each step forward brings you closer to realizing your small business aspirations.

Balancing Work and Family Life

Balancing work and family life is a delicate dance that many entrepreneurs, especially those managing small businesses, must master. The challenge lies in juggling the demands of a growing venture while nurturing meaningful connections with family members. In this section, we'll explore strategies to harmonize the responsibilities of work and family, ensuring both aspects of your life receive the attention they deserve.

Set clear boundaries between work and family time. Define specific hours for work and establish a routine that allows you to transition seamlessly between your professional and personal roles. Clearly communicate these boundaries to your family members and colleagues, fostering a mutual understanding of when you are available for work-related matters and when you are fully present for family engagements.

Prioritize tasks and responsibilities to avoid feeling overwhelmed. Create a realistic schedule that accommodates both work and family commitments. Identifying priorities allows you to allocate your time and energy efficiently, reducing stress and ensuring that essential tasks in both domains are addressed effectively. Recognize that not every task requires immediate attention, and it's okay to delegate or defer non-urgent responsibilities.

Establish a dedicated workspace that separates your professional and personal environments. Whether it's a home office, a co-working space, or a specific corner in your home, having a designated area for work helps create a mental boundary. When you're in your workspace, focus on work-related tasks, and when you step away, mentally transition to being fully present for your family.

Delegate tasks and responsibilities both at work and at home. Building a reliable support system allows you to share the workload and ensures that no single aspect of your life becomes overwhelming. Delegate specific tasks to team members at work, and involve family members in shared responsibilities at home. A collaborative approach not only lightens the load but also strengthens connections with those around you.

Practice effective time management by incorporating breaks and moments of relaxation into your schedule. Overworking can lead to burnout and strain your relationships. Schedule short breaks during the workday to recharge, and allocate dedicated family time without the intrusion of work-related distractions. These moments of respite are crucial for maintaining your well-being and fostering a healthy work-life balance.

Communicate openly with your family about your work commitments and goals. Transparency builds understanding and allows your family members to appreciate the significance of your professional endeavors. Share your schedule, discuss upcoming work-related events, and encourage open communication about how the family can support your entrepreneurial journey.

Establish realistic expectations for both work and family life. Acknowledge that there will be busy periods in your business that require additional focus, as well as times when family events take precedence. Setting realistic expectations helps manage everyone's expectations, minimizing disappointments and fostering a supportive environment.

Incorporate family into your entrepreneurial journey where possible. Share your successes and challenges with your family, involve them in decision-making processes when appropriate, and celebrate milestones together. This integration not only strengthens family bonds but also provides a deeper sense of purpose and shared accomplishment.

Lastly, be kind to yourself. Balancing work and family is an ongoing process, and it's normal to face occasional challenges. Understand that perfection is not the goal; rather, aim for a harmonious integration of your professional and personal life that aligns with your values and priorities.

In conclusion, achieving a balance between work and family life requires intentional efforts, clear communication, and a commitment to prioritizing what matters most. By setting boundaries, prioritizing tasks, creating dedicated workspaces, delegating responsibilities, practicing effective time management, communicating openly with your family, establishing realistic expectations, incorporating family into your journey, and being kind to yourself, you can navigate the intricate dance of entrepreneurship and family life with grace and fulfillment. Remember that finding this balance is a continuous journey, and each step forward contributes to the harmony of both work and family aspects of your life.

TIME MANAGEMENT STRATEGIES

Effective time management is the cornerstone of successfully balancing the demands of entrepreneurship and family life. In this section, we'll delve into practical strategies to help you make the most of your time, ensuring that both your professional and personal responsibilities are handled efficiently.

Firstly, recognize the power of prioritization. Not all tasks are created equal, and understanding which activities hold the most significance is essential. Prioritize tasks based on urgency, importance, and alignment with your overall goals. This strategic approach enables you to focus your time and energy on the tasks that have the most significant impact on your business and family life.

Create a daily or weekly schedule to structure your time effectively. Allocate specific time blocks for work-related tasks, family commitments, and personal activities. Having a clear schedule provides a visual roadmap for your day, helping you stay organized and ensuring that you allocate adequate time to both work and family responsibilities.

Leverage productivity tools and technology to streamline your workflow. Calendar apps, task management tools, and project management platforms can assist in organizing your schedule, setting reminders, and collaborating with team members. These tools can be invaluable in optimizing your time and ensuring that you stay on top of your professional and personal commitments.

Establish routines that foster efficiency. Routines create structure and automate certain aspects of your day, reducing decision fatigue and increasing productivity. Whether it's a morning routine to kickstart your day or an evening routine to wind down, having predictable patterns in your day allows you to navigate your responsibilities more smoothly.

Learn to say no when necessary. As an entrepreneur, opportunities and requests may flood your way. While it's tempting to say yes to everything, discernment is crucial. Assess each opportunity or request against your priorities and goals. Politely declining commitments that don't align with your overarching objectives allows you to maintain focus on what truly matters.

Implement the two-minute rule. If a task can be completed in two minutes or less, tackle it immediately. This rule helps prevent small tasks from accumulating and becoming overwhelming. Addressing quick tasks promptly frees up mental space and ensures that you stay on top of your responsibilities.

Practice the Pomodoro Technique or other time-blocking strategies. Breaking your work into focused, time-limited intervals with short breaks in between can enhance concentration and prevent burnout. By dedicating specific blocks of time to work, you create a balance that allows for focused productivity while maintaining opportunities for family and personal activities.

Minimize multitasking. While it may seem like a productivity booster, multitasking can lead to decreased efficiency and increased stress. Instead, focus on one task at a time, completing it before moving on to the next. This approach not only enhances the quality of your work but also allows you to be more present in your family engagements.

Regularly assess and adjust your time management strategies. The demands of entrepreneurship and family life are dynamic, requiring flexibility in your approach. Regularly evaluate the effectiveness of your time management strategies and be open to adjusting them based on changes in your business or personal life.

Finally, practice self-care to maintain your overall well-being. Adequate rest, regular exercise, and moments of relaxation contribute to increased energy levels and improved focus. Taking care of yourself ensures that you have the stamina and resilience to manage both your professional and family responsibilities effectively.

In conclusion, effective time management is a foundational skill for entrepreneurs seeking to balance work and family life. By prioritizing tasks, creating schedules, leveraging productivity tools, establishing routines, learning to say no, implementing time-blocking strategies, minimizing multitasking, regularly assessing strategies, and practicing self-care, you can optimize your time and create a harmonious integration of your professional and personal responsibilities. Remember that time is a valuable resource, and managing it wisely allows you to navigate the intricate dance of entrepreneurship and family life with greater ease and fulfillment.

CREATING A FLEXIBLE SCHEDULE

Creating a flexible schedule is a key strategy for entrepreneurs aiming to strike a balance between the demands of their businesses and family life. Flexibility is the cornerstone of adaptability, allowing you to navigate the dynamic landscape of entrepreneurship while ensuring you can be present for the various aspects of your personal life.

Start by embracing the concept of fluidity in your schedule. Recognize that the rigid nine-to-five structure may not always align with the unpredictable nature of entrepreneurship and family responsibilities. Embracing flexibility means understanding that certain days may require a different distribution of your time and energy.

One approach to a flexible schedule is adopting a block scheduling method. Instead of adhering strictly to fixed hours for work and family time, divide your day into blocks. Assign specific blocks of time to work-related tasks, family commitments, and personal activities. This approach provides a framework that accommodates the fluid nature of entrepreneurship, allowing you to allocate time based on the unique demands of each day.

Another aspect of creating a flexible schedule involves setting realistic expectations. While planning is crucial, it's equally important to recognize that unexpected challenges or opportunities may arise. Building buffer time into your schedule allows you to address unforeseen circumstances without derailing your entire day. This flexibility enables you to adapt to the ebb and flow of entrepreneurship while maintaining a sense of control over your time.

Communicate openly with your team, clients, and family members about your flexible schedule. Transparency fosters understanding and ensures that those involved are aware of the times when you may be more or less available. Set clear expectations regarding response times and availability, providing a realistic perspective on your schedule and reinforcing the importance of adaptability in your professional and personal life.

Consider integrating a dedicated 'flex day' into your week. This is a day where you have the flexibility to address both work and family needs without the constraints of a rigid schedule. Use this day to catch up on tasks, attend family events, or pursue personal activities. Having a designated flex day acknowledges the unpredictable nature of entrepreneurship while providing a structured approach to balancing your commitments.

Explore the benefits of remote work if applicable to your business. Remote work allows for greater flexibility in managing your time and location. It can be particularly advantageous for entrepreneurs who need to balance business tasks with family responsibilities. Discuss remote work options with your team and assess how this flexibility can contribute to a more balanced and integrated lifestyle.

Incorporate designated breaks and downtime into your flexible schedule. Taking short breaks throughout the day allows you to recharge and maintain focus, while intentional downtime provides opportunities for relaxation and family engagement. Building these moments of respite into your schedule contributes to your overall well-being and prevents burnout.

Lastly, periodically evaluate the effectiveness of your flexible schedule. Assess whether it aligns with your evolving business needs and family dynamics. Solicit feedback from team members, clients, and family members to ensure that the flexibility you've incorporated is contributing positively to both your professional and personal life.

In conclusion, creating a flexible schedule is a dynamic and intentional approach to managing the demands of entrepreneurship and family life. By embracing fluidity, adopting block scheduling, setting realistic expectations, communicating openly, integrating a flex day, exploring remote work options, incorporating breaks and downtime, and evaluating effectiveness, you can design a schedule that aligns with the unique challenges and opportunities of your entrepreneurial journey. Remember that flexibility is a strength that allows you to navigate the complexities of both work and family with resilience and fulfillment.

Chapter 11

Chapter 11: Retirement Planning

Welcome to Chapter 11: Retirement Planning, a crucial aspect of securing your financial future and ensuring a comfortable and fulfilling retirement. In this chapter, we'll explore the importance of early retirement planning, the various retirement accounts available, and strategic approaches to building a nest egg that can sustain you during your golden years.

Retirement is a significant milestone, and preparing for it requires thoughtful consideration and proactive financial decisions. Whether you're just starting your career or you're a seasoned professional, understanding the essentials of retirement planning empowers you to make informed choices that align with your long-term goals.

We'll dive into the key elements of retirement planning, unraveling the complexities to provide you with a clear roadmap. From exploring retirement account options like 401(k)s and IRAs to understanding the impact of inflation on your retirement savings, this chapter is designed to equip you with the knowledge needed to make prudent decisions for your financial well-being.

As you embark on this journey, envision the retirement lifestyle you desire. Whether it involves travel, pursuing hobbies, or spending quality time with loved ones, effective retirement planning lays the foundation for turning those dreams into reality. We'll guide you through the steps to assess your current financial standing, set realistic retirement goals, and implement strategies to accumulate the funds necessary to enjoy the retirement you've envisioned.

Remember, retirement planning is not a one-size-fits-all endeavor. Your unique circumstances, goals, and aspirations will shape the path you take. By delving into the insights provided in this chapter, you'll gain the tools to navigate the intricacies of retirement planning, ensuring that your later years are marked by financial security and the ability to relish the fruits of your lifelong labor.

Let's embark on the journey of securing a retirement that reflects your aspirations and provides the peace of mind you deserve. Whether retirement is on the horizon or a distant destination, the knowledge gained in this chapter will serve as a valuable compass, guiding you toward a future filled with financial stability and the freedom to savor life after your working years.

The Importance of Retirement Savings

As you navigate the chapters of your financial journey, few destinations are as significant as retirement. Chapter 11, aptly titled "The Importance of Retirement Savings," sheds light on why planning for your golden years is a critical aspect of your overall financial well-being.

Imagine reaching a point in your life where the hustle and bustle of the daily grind takes a back seat, allowing you to savor the fruits of your labor and embrace a more leisurely pace. This idyllic picture of retirement is what many aspire to, and yet, it requires thoughtful preparation.

One of the paramount reasons retirement savings are crucial lies in the changing landscape of work and income during retirement. Unlike your working years where a steady paycheck sustains your lifestyle, retirement signals a shift in income sources. Social Security benefits and pensions may form part of your income, but having a robust retirement savings cushion becomes indispensable to maintain the quality of life you desire.

Moreover, the increasing life expectancy of the population adds another layer of significance to retirement savings. With longer life spans, the funds you accumulate must not only sustain you but also provide for a potentially extended period of retirement. A well-padded retirement savings account ensures that you can enjoy your later years without the specter of financial strain.

Retirement savings act as a financial safety net, offering you peace of mind and security. Life is inherently unpredictable, and unexpected expenses or health-related challenges can arise. Having a dedicated pool of savings specifically earmarked for retirement allows you to face these uncertainties with confidence, knowing that you've diligently prepared for the unknown.

Another compelling reason to prioritize retirement savings is the impact of inflation. Over time, the cost of living tends to rise, diminishing the purchasing power of your money. By consistently contributing to your retirement savings, you're essentially safeguarding your funds against the erosive effects of inflation, ensuring that your savings can meet the future costs of living.

Additionally, retirement savings empower you to maintain a degree of financial independence during your later years. Instead of relying solely on external sources for financial support, having a well-managed retirement portfolio allows you to make choices aligned with your preferences and priorities.

For those who dream of a retirement filled with travel, pursuing hobbies, or even starting a new venture, robust retirement savings provide the means to turn those dreams into reality. The freedom to structure your retirement years in a way that brings you joy and fulfillment is a priceless aspect of effective retirement planning.

In conclusion, the importance of retirement savings cannot be overstated. It is a foundational element of securing a future that aligns with your aspirations and offers financial stability. By understanding the shifting dynamics of income, the impact of increasing life expectancy, the need for a financial safety net, the challenge of inflation, and the pursuit of independence and fulfillment, you lay the groundwork for a retirement that is not just an endpoint but a vibrant and enriching chapter of your life. So, let's delve further into the strategies and considerations that make retirement savings a cornerstone of financial success.

UNDERSTANDING RETIREMENT ACCOUNTS

Navigating the landscape of retirement planning involves understanding the diverse array of retirement accounts available to you. In this exploration, we'll delve into the significance of these accounts and how they can be instrumental in shaping your financial future.

Retirement accounts serve as dedicated vessels for accumulating funds specifically earmarked for your post-work years. One of the most common retirement accounts is the 401(k), often offered by employers. This employer-sponsored plan allows you to contribute a portion of your pre-tax income, enabling you to reduce your taxable income while building a substantial nest egg for retirement. Some employers may even match your contributions, amplifying the growth potential of your savings.

Individuals also have the option of opening an Individual Retirement Account (IRA). IRAs come in different varieties, each with its own set of rules and benefits. Traditional IRAs allow you to make tax-deductible contributions, while Roth IRAs involve contributing after-tax dollars, with the advantage of tax-free withdrawals in retirement. These accounts offer flexibility and can be tailored to your specific financial circumstances and goals.

Another retirement account worth exploring is the Simplified Employee Pension (SEP) IRA, which is often favored by self-employed individuals and small business owners. The SEP IRA allows for tax-deductible contributions, making it an attractive option for those with variable income streams.

Understanding the mechanics of these retirement accounts is paramount because they provide distinct tax advantages and contribute to the overall diversification of your retirement portfolio. By leveraging these accounts effectively, you not only maximize your tax benefits but also harness the power of compounding to grow your savings over time.

Moreover, retirement accounts are designed to encourage disciplined saving by offering penalties for early withdrawals. While this may seem restrictive, it serves the crucial purpose of ensuring that your retirement funds remain untouched until you genuinely need them. This protective measure reinforces the long-term nature of retirement savings, discouraging impulsive decisions that could jeopardize your financial security in later years.

As you navigate the nuances of retirement accounts, it's essential to stay informed about contribution limits, eligibility criteria, and any changes in tax laws that may impact these accounts. Regularly reviewing and adjusting your contributions in accordance with your financial circumstances and goals ensures that you are making the most of the benefits offered by these accounts.

In conclusion, understanding retirement accounts is akin to wielding a powerful tool in your financial toolkit. It empowers you to make informed decisions, capitalize on tax advantages, and create a diversified and resilient retirement portfolio. By recognizing the unique features of accounts like 401(k)s, IRAs, and SEP IRAs, you set the stage for a retirement strategy that aligns with your aspirations and provides the financial security you deserve. As we continue our journey through retirement planning, let's explore how these accounts can be strategically utilized to sculpt a retirement that reflects your vision for the future.

PLANNING FOR RETIREMENT AS A MOM

As a mom, planning for retirement brings its own set of considerations and intricacies, yet it is a vital undertaking that sets the stage for a future of financial security and the ability to relish the rewards of your hard work. In this exploration of retirement planning tailored to moms, we'll delve into the unique aspects that should be taken into account as you chart the course for your post-work years.

One of the central elements for moms in retirement planning is the often multifaceted nature of their roles. Balancing the responsibilities of caregiving, managing a household, and potentially juggling a career can make it challenging to allocate time and attention to long-term financial planning. Nevertheless, recognizing the importance of securing your financial future is the first step toward creating a retirement strategy that aligns with your goals.

For moms who have taken breaks from the workforce or opted for part-time work to prioritize family, the impact on retirement savings may be a consideration. In such scenarios, exploring retirement accounts that offer flexibility becomes crucial. Roth IRAs, for instance, allow for tax-free withdrawals in retirement and can be particularly advantageous for those with variable income streams or intermittent employment.

It's also essential for moms to factor in the financial implications of potential career interruptions, such as taking time off to raise children. While these breaks are immensely valuable, they can impact the overall trajectory of retirement savings. Exploring avenues to continue contributing to retirement accounts during these periods or strategically re-entering the workforce can help mitigate potential gaps in savings.

For moms who are the primary breadwinners or share financial responsibilities with a partner, open communication about retirement goals and strategies is paramount. Aligning your visions for retirement, discussing contribution plans, and collectively navigating financial decisions can enhance your ability to reach shared retirement aspirations.

Furthermore, as a mom, your retirement planning may extend beyond your individual needs to encompass the financial well-being of your children. This might involve saving for their education or factoring potential support into your retirement budget. Creating a holistic plan that considers both your personal aspirations and the needs of your family ensures a comprehensive and well-rounded approach to retirement planning.

It's also worth acknowledging the emotional and psychological aspects of retirement planning for moms. The prospect of an empty nest or transitioning to a different phase of life can evoke a range of emotions. Recognizing and addressing these feelings, seeking support from loved ones, and, if necessary, consulting with a financial advisor or counselor can contribute to a more holistic and balanced approach to retirement planning.

In conclusion, planning for retirement as a mom is a dynamic and multifaceted journey that requires consideration of unique circumstances and aspirations. By recognizing the impact of caregiving roles, exploring flexible retirement account options, maintaining open communication with your partner, addressing potential career interruptions, and considering the financial needs of your family, you pave the way for a retirement that reflects your values and priorities. As we continue our exploration of retirement planning, let's delve further into the strategies and considerations that make retirement a fulfilling and well-prepared chapter of your life.

Strategies for Catching Up on Retirement Savings

For many individuals, the realization that they may need to catch up on retirement savings often comes with a mix of concern and determination. Life is filled with twists and turns, and sometimes, despite our best intentions, the path to retirement may not unfold as planned. However, the good news is that there are various strategies and approaches that can help you make up for lost time and bolster your retirement savings. In this exploration, we'll delve into these strategies with a focus on practical steps and a positive mindset.

The first and foremost step in catching up on retirement savings is to assess your current financial situation and set realistic goals. This involves taking a close look at your existing retirement accounts, evaluating your expenses, and determining how much you can comfortably allocate toward savings. While catching up may require adjustments and sacrifices, having a clear understanding of your financial landscape is a crucial starting point.

Consider maximizing contributions to retirement accounts. If you're eligible, contributing the maximum allowed amount to employer-sponsored plans like 401(k)s or individual plans like IRAs can significantly accelerate the growth of your retirement nest egg. Take advantage of catch-up contributions, which allow individuals aged 50 and older to contribute additional funds beyond the standard limits.

Exploring diversified investment strategies is another avenue for catching up on retirement savings. While investments inherently come with risks, a diversified portfolio tailored to your risk tolerance and time horizon can potentially yield higher returns. Consulting with a financial advisor can provide valuable insights into creating an investment strategy aligned with your goals.

Delaying retirement is a pragmatic approach for those looking to catch up on savings. By extending your working years, you not only continue to earn income but also delay the need to tap into your retirement funds. This extra time in the workforce allows your savings to potentially grow, and you may even be able to contribute more during these additional working years.

Consider strategic career moves that boost your income. This might involve negotiating a higher salary, seeking promotions, or exploring job opportunities with more lucrative compensation packages. While these steps may require effort and initiative, they can have a direct impact on your ability to save more for retirement.

Downsizing your lifestyle is a practical consideration when playing catch-up on retirement savings. Evaluate your current expenses, identify areas where you can cut back, and redirect those funds into your retirement accounts. While downsizing may involve some adjustments, the long-term benefits of bolstered retirement savings can outweigh short-term sacrifices.

Lastly, seeking professional guidance can be invaluable. Financial advisors can assess your individual situation, help you navigate investment options, and tailor a strategy that aligns with your goals. Their expertise can provide clarity and confidence as you work toward catching up on retirement savings.

In conclusion, catching up on retirement savings is a realistic and achievable goal with thoughtful planning and strategic approaches. By assessing your current situation, maximizing contributions, diversifying investments, delaying retirement, boosting income, downsizing expenses, and seeking professional advice, you can take proactive steps toward securing a more robust financial future. As we continue our exploration of retirement strategies, let's delve deeper into the specific tactics and considerations that empower you to catch up on savings and embark on a path of financial well-being.

CATCH-UP CONTRIBUTIONS

Catch-up contributions are a powerful tool in the arsenal of individuals who find themselves behind on their retirement savings. Recognizing the challenges and unique circumstances that can lead to a shortfall in retirement preparedness, policy-makers have introduced catch-up contributions to provide an avenue for individuals aged 50 and older to supercharge their retirement savings. In this exploration, we'll delve into the significance of catch-up contributions, the mechanics of how they work, and the strategic considerations for maximizing their benefits.

The concept of catch-up contributions emerged from a recognition that individuals closer to retirement may face increased financial responsibilities, such as caring for aging parents or covering higher education costs for children. These added financial burdens can limit the capacity to save for retirement. To address this, the Internal Revenue Service (IRS) introduced catch-up contributions, allowing individuals aged 50 and above to contribute additional funds to their retirement accounts beyond the standard limits.

One of the primary benefits of catch-up contributions is their potential to significantly boost the overall value of your retirement portfolio. For employer-sponsored plans, such as

401(k)s, individuals aged 50 and older can contribute an additional amount on top of the standard annual limit. This extra contribution can enhance the growth potential of your retirement savings, especially when considering the compounding effect over the remaining years until retirement.

The catch-up contribution limit is subject to adjustment by the IRS based on economic factors. As of my last knowledge update in January 2022, individuals aged 50 and older could contribute an additional $6,500 to their 401(k) plans and an extra $1,000 to their individual retirement accounts (IRAs) beyond the standard limits. It's important to stay informed about any changes to these limits, as they may be adjusted periodically.

Understanding the mechanics of catch-up contributions involves knowing the standard contribution limits and how the catch-up amounts fit into the overall framework. For example, the standard contribution limit for 401(k) plans in 2022 was $19,500 for individuals under 50. With catch-up contributions, those aged 50 and above could contribute a total of $26,000. Similarly, for IRAs, the standard limit was $6,000 in 2022, with a catch-up contribution limit of $7,000 for individuals aged 50 and older.

Strategically incorporating catch-up contributions into your retirement planning requires a thoughtful assessment of your financial situation and goals. If you find yourself behind on your retirement savings, taking full advantage of catch-up contributions can be a game-changer. Consider consulting with a financial advisor to determine the optimal amount for catch-up contributions based on your individual circumstances.

It's worth noting that catch-up contributions are not a one-size-fits-all solution, and their effectiveness depends on various factors, including your overall financial picture, investment strategy, and retirement timeline. Additionally, catch-up contributions are subject to annual limits set by the IRS, and exceeding these limits can result in penalties.

In conclusion, catch-up contributions offer a valuable opportunity for individuals aged 50 and older to accelerate their retirement savings. By understanding the benefits, staying informed about contribution limits, and incorporating catch-up contributions strategically into your retirement plan, you can enhance the likelihood of achieving your financial goals in retirement. As we continue our exploration of retirement planning, let's delve deeper into specific strategies and considerations for optimizing catch-up contributions and navigating the path toward a secure and fulfilling retirement.

INVESTING FOR RETIREMENT SECURITY

Investing for retirement security is a multifaceted journey that involves thoughtful consideration of various factors, from risk tolerance to time horizon. As individuals approach the prospect of retirement, the focus of their investment strategy often shifts from accumulation to preservation and income generation. In this exploration, we'll delve into the key aspects of investing for retirement security, emphasizing the importance of a balanced and diversified approach.

One of the foundational principles of investing for retirement security is understanding the dynamics of risk and return. While the potential for higher returns often accompanies higher levels of risk, individuals nearing retirement typically seek a more balanced approach. Preservation of capital becomes paramount, and the emphasis may shift towards income-producing investments that offer stability and a reliable stream of returns.

Diversification remains a linchpin in the strategy for retirement security. Spreading investments across a variety of asset classes—such as stocks, bonds, and real estate—helps mitigate risks associated with any single investment category. The goal is to create a resilient portfolio that can weather market fluctuations while still delivering a satisfactory return on investment. A diversified approach also allows retirees to tap into different sources of income, contributing to financial stability in retirement.

Income-generating investments, such as dividend-paying stocks and bonds, play a crucial role in the retirement security equation. Dividend stocks can provide a steady stream of income, and bonds offer regular interest payments. The combination of these income sources can create a reliable cash flow to cover living expenses during retirement. Additionally, carefully selected dividend-paying stocks with a history of consistent payouts may offer the potential for capital appreciation over time.

Another consideration in the quest for retirement security is the concept of a glide path. This involves gradually adjusting the asset allocation of a portfolio as one moves closer to retirement. Early in the retirement planning journey, a portfolio may have a higher allocation to growth-oriented investments. However, as retirement approaches, the focus shifts towards more conservative investments to protect accumulated wealth.

Engaging with a financial advisor becomes particularly valuable when navigating the nuances of retirement investing. A professional advisor can help individuals define their risk tolerance, identify suitable investment vehicles, and craft a personalized strategy that aligns with their financial goals. This partnership provides ongoing guidance and adjustments, ensuring that the investment plan remains in sync with the individual's evolving needs.

The impact of inflation on retirement security cannot be overstated. While fixed-income investments may provide stability, they can be vulnerable to the eroding effects of inflation over time. Incorporating inflation-hedging strategies, such as investments with the potential for capital appreciation,

becomes essential in maintaining purchasing power throughout retirement.

Regular reviews and adjustments to the investment portfolio are integral to the strategy for retirement security. Market
conditions, economic trends, and personal circumstances may
change, necessitating periodic evaluations and tweaks to the
investment plan. Staying informed about the performance of
investments and being willing to make adjustments when
needed contribute to a resilient and adaptive approach to retirement investing.

In conclusion, investing for retirement security involves a
dynamic and strategic approach that considers risk tolerance,
diversification, income generation, and the impact of inflation.
As individuals transition from the accumulation phase to the
preservation phase, a balanced and well-diversified portfolio,
coupled with income-generating investments, can contribute
to a secure and fulfilling retirement. Engaging with a financial
advisor and staying attuned to the evolving landscape of retirement planning further enhances the likelihood of achieving
long-term financial security.

Chapter 12

Chapter 12: Real Estate and Homeownership

Welcome to the twelfth chapter of our journey towards financial empowerment and security. In this installment, we turn our attention to the realm of real estate and homeownership—an integral component of many individuals' financial landscapes. The prospect of owning a home is not just about having a place to live; it's a cornerstone of financial strategy, offering opportunities for wealth building, stability, and a sense of belonging.

For many, owning a home represents a significant milestone, a symbol of accomplishment and a tangible investment in the future. This chapter explores the multifaceted aspects of real estate, delving into the benefits of homeownership, strategic considerations for buying or selling property, and the role of real estate in a comprehensive financial plan.

We'll unravel the intricacies of the real estate market, discussing how market conditions can influence buying and selling decisions. Understanding the nuances of real estate transactions empowers individuals to make informed choices aligned with their financial goals.

Beyond the financial aspects, we'll explore the emotional and psychological dimensions of homeownership. A home is not just a piece of property; it's a haven, a place where memories are made, and families grow. Balancing the emotional and financial aspects of homeownership is a delicate dance, and this chapter provides insights to navigate this intersection.

Moreover, we'll examine the potential for real estate as an investment. From rental properties to real estate investment trusts (REITs), the chapter offers a comprehensive overview of how real estate can be a dynamic component of an investment portfolio.

As we embark on this exploration of real estate and home-ownership, the goal is to equip you with the knowledge and tools to make sound decisions in this critical area of personal finance. Whether you're a first-time homebuyer, a seasoned homeowner, or someone considering real estate as an invest-ment avenue, this chapter will provide valuable insights to guide you on your journey towards financial well-being. Let's dive into the world of real estate, where homes become more than just structures—they become the foundation for financial security and the backdrop for life's most meaningful moments.

Evaluating the Pros and Cons of Homeownership

The decision to embark on the journey of homeownership is a momentous one, carrying both emotional and financial weight. As you stand at the crossroads of renting and owning, it's essential to weigh the pros and cons carefully to make an informed choice aligned with your current lifestyle, future aspirations, and financial goals.

Pros of Homeownership:

1. **Building Equity:** One of the primary advantages of owning a home is the opportunity to build equity. Unlike renting, where monthly payments contribute solely to the landlord's wealth, mortgage payments gradually increase your ownership stake in the property.
2. **Stability and Security:** Homeownership provides a sense of stability and security. Knowing that you have a place to call your own can bring peace of mind and a feeling of permanence.
3. **Personalization and Control:** When you own a home, you have the freedom to personalize and modify it according to your tastes and needs. From painting the walls to landscaping the backyard, you have control over your living space.
4. **Potential for Appreciation:** Real estate has the potential to appreciate over time, building additional wealth for homeowners. While market conditions vary, historically, real estate values have tended to increase.
5. **Tax Benefits:** Homeownership often comes with tax advantages. Mortgage interest and property tax deductions can contribute to significant savings during tax season.

Cons of Homeownership:

1. **Financial Commitment:** Owning a home involves a substantial financial commitment. Beyond the down payment, there are mortgage payments, property taxes, insurance, and maintenance costs to consider.
2. **Limited Flexibility:** Homeownership can limit geographic and job-related flexibility. If you need to relocate for work or personal reasons, selling a home can be a complex and time-consuming process.
3. **Maintenance Responsibilities:** Unlike renting, where landlords handle maintenance and repairs, homeowners

are responsible for the upkeep of their properties. Maintenance costs can add up, especially for unexpected repairs.

4. **Market Fluctuations:** Real estate markets can be unpredictable, and property values may fluctuate. Economic downturns or local market conditions can impact the resale value of your home.

5. **Upfront Costs:** The initial costs of homeownership, including the down payment, closing costs, and other fees, can be a significant barrier for many individuals. Saving for these expenses is a crucial part of the homebuying process.

Navigating the Decision:

As you evaluate the pros and cons of homeownership, it's crucial to assess your current financial situation, future goals, and lifestyle preferences. Consider factors such as job stability, desired location, and your willingness to commit to the responsibilities of homeownership.

Homeownership is a substantial and meaningful investment, but it's not a one-size-fits-all solution. Carefully weighing the advantages and disadvantages will empower you to make a decision that aligns with your unique circumstances and aspirations. Remember that each individual's journey is unique, and homeownership is a milestone that should enhance your life and financial well-being.

FINANCIAL CONSIDERATIONS FOR BUYING A HOME

When venturing into the realm of homeownership, a key aspect is understanding the financial considerations associated with this significant decision. Buying a home involves more than finding the perfect property; it requires a thorough assessment of your financial readiness and a clear understanding of the costs involved.

First and foremost, it's essential to evaluate your credit-worthiness. A strong credit score is a valuable asset when applying for a mortgage. Lenders use your credit history to determine the interest rate and loan terms. Before starting the homebuying process, obtain a copy of your credit report, review it for accuracy, and address any discrepancies. Taking steps to improve your credit score, if necessary, can have a positive impact on your mortgage options.

Down payment requirements are another critical factor. While it's possible to secure a mortgage with a down payment as low as 3% or 5%, a larger down payment can offer advantages such as lower monthly payments and reduced interest costs over the life of the loan. Consider your financial situation and aim for a down payment that aligns with your budget and goals.

Beyond the down payment, it's crucial to factor in closing costs. Closing costs typically include fees for loan origination, appraisal, title insurance, and other services. These costs can add up to several thousand dollars, so it's important to budget accordingly. Some homebuyers negotiate with sellers to cover a portion of the closing costs, but this is not guaranteed.

Understanding the total cost of homeownership is paramount. In addition to the mortgage payment, homeowners must budget for property taxes, homeowners insurance, and possibly private mortgage insurance (PMI) if the down payment is less than 20%. Property taxes vary by location, and it's essential to research the rates in the area where you plan to buy.

Maintenance and repair expenses are often underestimated by first-time homebuyers. Unlike renting, where landlords handle these costs, homeowners are responsible for maintaining their properties. Creating a fund for ongoing maintenance and unforeseen repairs is a wise financial strategy. This fund can mitigate the financial impact of unexpected issues such as a leaky roof or a malfunctioning HVAC system.

Interest rates play a significant role in the overall cost of homeownership. Mortgage interest rates can fluctuate based on economic conditions and other factors. Monitoring interest rate trends and choosing an optimal time to lock in your rate can result in substantial savings over the life of your mortgage.

Lastly, it's essential to assess your overall financial health and stability. Consider factors such as job security, future income potential, and potential life changes. Homeownership is a long-term commitment, and ensuring that you are financially prepared for this journey is crucial.

In conclusion, the financial considerations for buying a home extend beyond the purchase price. Thoroughly examining your creditworthiness, down payment options, closing costs, ongoing expenses, and overall financial stability will position you for a successful and sustainable homeownership experience. Approach the process with a clear understanding of your financial picture, and you'll be better equipped to make informed decisions that align with your long-term goals.

ALTERNATIVE HOUSING OPTIONS

While traditional homeownership is a common aspiration, alternative housing options have gained popularity for those seeking flexibility, affordability, or unique living experiences. Exploring these alternatives can provide a broader perspective on the possibilities available in the housing market.

One notable alternative is renting. Renting offers flexibility, making it an attractive option for individuals who are not ready to commit to a long-term investment. Renters have the freedom to explore different neighborhoods, cities, or even countries without the responsibilities associated with homeownership. Moreover, renting often includes maintenance services provided by landlords, relieving tenants of the burden of property upkeep.

Co-living is another emerging trend in alternative housing. This arrangement involves individuals or families sharing living spaces, creating a sense of community while also reducing living expenses. Co-living spaces often come fully furnished and may include shared amenities, promoting social interaction among residents. This option is particularly popular in urban areas where housing costs are high, offering a solution for those seeking affordability and a sense of community.

Tiny houses have captured the imagination of individuals looking to downsize and simplify their lives. These compact dwellings, often ranging from 100 to 400 square feet, emphasize efficient use of space and minimalistic living. Tiny house living is not only a response to rising housing costs but also a lifestyle choice for those who value sustainability and a smaller environmental footprint.

Mobile and manufactured homes present an affordable housing option that combines homeownership with mobility. These homes, built off-site and transported to their location, offer a more budget-friendly alternative compared to traditional houses. They can be an excellent choice for those seeking homeownership without the financial commitment of a traditional mortgage.

Additionally, the rise of the digital nomad lifestyle has given way to unconventional housing options such as house-sitting and home-sharing. House-sitting involves individuals caring for someone else's home while the owner is away, providing free accommodation in exchange for house maintenance. Home-sharing platforms connect homeowners with individuals seeking temporary accommodation, fostering a sharing economy within the housing sector.

It's important to note that while alternative housing options offer unique advantages, they may come with their own set of challenges. Renters may face the uncertainty of lease renewals, co-living dynamics require effective communication and compatibility among residents, and tiny house living demands a deliberate approach to decluttering and simplifying one's possessions.

Ultimately, the decision between traditional homeownership and alternative options depends on individual preferences, financial considerations, and lifestyle priorities. Each choice has its merits, and exploring the diverse landscape of housing options allows individuals to align their living arrangements with their unique circumstances and aspirations. Whether opting for a tiny house, co-living space, or mobile home, the variety of alternatives enriches the housing market, providing individuals with the opportunity to find a home that truly suits their needs and enhances their quality of life.

Building Home Equity

Homeownership is not just about having a place to call your own; it's also a pathway to building wealth through home equity. Home equity represents the portion of your property that you truly own, calculated by subtracting the outstanding mortgage balance from the property's market value. As you make mortgage payments and property values appreciate, your home equity grows, offering financial benefits and opportunities.

One of the primary ways to build home equity is through consistent mortgage payments. Each payment made toward the principal balance contributes to increasing your equity stake in the property. Over time, as the outstanding loan amount decreases, your ownership share grows. Making extra payments or paying more than the required monthly amount accelerates this process, helping you build equity at a faster pace.

Property value appreciation is another factor influencing home equity. When the real estate market experiences growth, the value of your home can increase. This appreciation contributes to an automatic gain in equity, even without additional mortgage payments. Engaging in home improvement projects that enhance the property's appeal and functionality can also positively impact its market value, further boosting your equity.

Taking advantage of a shorter mortgage term can be a strategic approach to build home equity rapidly. While 30-year mortgages are common, opting for a 15 or 20-year mortgage shortens the repayment period, allowing you to build equity more quickly. Although monthly payments may be higher, the overall interest paid over the life of the loan is significantly reduced.

Home equity can serve as a valuable financial resource through options like home equity loans and lines of credit. These financial instruments allow homeowners to borrow against the equity they've accumulated. Whether for home improvements, debt consolidation, or other financial needs, tapping into home equity provides a cost-effective borrowing solution compared to other forms of credit.

For those who aspire to increase their home equity systematically, making strategic home improvements is key. Renovations that enhance the property's functionality, energy efficiency, or aesthetic appeal not only contribute to increased market value but also provide a higher quality of living. From kitchen upgrades to energy-efficient installations, these improvements add both immediate and long-term value.

It's crucial to monitor the local real estate market trends to stay informed about the potential for property value appreciation. Being aware of the economic factors influencing housing prices allows homeowners to make informed decisions about their property and overall financial strategy.

Building home equity is a gradual process that requires financial discipline, strategic planning, and a long-term perspective. Whether through regular mortgage payments, property appreciation, or intentional home improvements, homeowners have the opportunity to accumulate wealth and financial security over time. Homeownership, when approached thoughtfully, not only fulfills the dream of having a place to call home but also becomes a cornerstone for building a stable and prosperous financial future.

HOMEOWNERSHIP AS AN INVESTMENT

Owning a home is often considered one of life's significant milestones, a place to create memories and build a sense of stability. Beyond its emotional value, homeownership is also a powerful financial investment that can provide numerous benefits and contribute to long-term wealth creation.

One of the key advantages of homeownership as an investment is the potential for property appreciation. Real estate markets generally exhibit a tendency to appreciate over time, although the rate of appreciation can vary based on location and economic conditions. When you purchase a home in a desirable neighborhood or an area experiencing growth, the value of your property may increase, resulting in a potential profit when you decide to sell.

Equity accumulation is another compelling aspect of homeownership as an investment. With each mortgage payment, you're not only covering the cost of living in your home but also building equity, the portion of your property that you truly own. As the outstanding loan balance decreases and property values rise, your equity stake grows, providing a source of financial security and flexibility.

The tax benefits associated with homeownership add another layer of financial advantage. Mortgage interest payments and property tax payments are often tax-deductible, reducing your overall tax liability. These deductions can result in significant savings, especially during the early years of homeownership when mortgage interest payments are typically higher.

Homeownership also serves as a hedge against inflation. Unlike renting, where monthly payments may increase with inflation, homeowners with fixed-rate mortgages enjoy a stable mortgage payment throughout the life of the loan. This means that as the cost of living rises, your housing expenses remain relatively constant, contributing to increased financial stability over time.

For many families, a home represents a form of forced savings. The monthly mortgage payment becomes a disciplined way to set aside money for the future, building wealth gradually. This forced savings approach can be especially beneficial for individuals who may struggle to consistently save money through other means.

Moreover, homeownership provides a degree of control over your living space. Unlike renting, where landlords can impose restrictions and rent increases, owning a home allows you to make decisions about property modifications, landscaping, and other improvements that can enhance both your quality of life and the property's value.

As an investment, homeownership is not without risks. Economic downturns, fluctuations in the real estate market, and unexpected maintenance costs can impact the financial returns on your investment. However, by approaching homeownership with careful consideration, staying informed about market trends, and making strategic decisions, these risks can be minimized.

In conclusion, homeownership is a multifaceted investment that extends beyond the emotional and practical aspects of having a place to call home. It has the potential to generate wealth through property appreciation, equity accumulation, tax benefits, and the stability it offers in an inflationary environment. For those seeking a long-term financial strategy, homeownership remains a cornerstone of building financial security and achieving lasting prosperity.

MAINTENANCE AND COST CONSIDERATIONS

While homeownership offers numerous financial advantages and the potential for building equity, it's essential to recognize the responsibilities that come with maintaining a property. Successfully navigating these aspects will contribute to the long-term success of your investment and ensure your home remains a valuable asset.

One of the key considerations in homeownership is ongoing maintenance. Regular upkeep is crucial to preserving the condition and value of your property. This includes tasks such as routine cleaning, landscaping, and addressing minor repairs promptly. By staying proactive in maintaining your home, you can prevent small issues from escalating into more significant problems that could potentially lead to costly repairs.

Understanding the lifespan of various components in your home is also essential for effective maintenance planning. Items like the roof, heating and cooling systems, and appliances have finite lifespans and may require replacement or major repairs over time. Creating a maintenance schedule that aligns with these lifespans can help you anticipate and budget for future expenses, preventing financial strain when replacements are necessary.

Budgeting for maintenance costs is a critical aspect of responsible homeownership. While mortgage payments provide a sense of stability, homeowners must also account for additional expenses related to property upkeep. Setting aside funds for both routine maintenance and unexpected repairs ensures you're financially prepared for the inevitable wear and tear that comes with homeownership.

Homeowners should also be mindful of property taxes and insurance costs, which can fluctuate based on local regulations and market conditions. Staying informed about potential increases in property taxes and periodically reviewing your insurance coverage can help you anticipate changes in these ongoing expenses.

Energy efficiency is another aspect of homeownership that can impact long-term costs. Investing in energy-efficient appliances, windows, and insulation not only reduces your environmental footprint but can also lead to lower utility bills. Making informed decisions about energy efficiency during the home purchase process or as part of renovations can contribute to long-term cost savings.

Unexpected financial challenges may arise, such as emergency repairs or sudden changes in income. Establishing an emergency fund specific to homeownership can provide a financial safety net during these times. This fund can be used to cover unexpected repairs or mortgage payments in the event of a temporary financial setback, helping to safeguard your home and financial well-being.

In summary, homeownership involves ongoing responsibilities and costs that extend beyond the initial purchase. Proactive maintenance, understanding the lifespan of home components, budgeting for ongoing expenses, and addressing energy efficiency can contribute to the overall financial health of your investment. By approaching homeownership with a comprehensive understanding of these considerations, you can navigate the challenges and enjoy the long-term benefits of property ownership.

Chapter 13

Chapter 13: Legacy and Wealth Transfer

Welcome to Chapter 13: Legacy and Wealth Transfer, a crucial segment of our journey toward financial empowerment. As we navigate the intricate landscape of personal finance, it becomes increasingly important to consider the legacy we leave behind and the methods through which we transfer our wealth to future generations. This chapter delves into the strategies, considerations, and mindful approaches that can help you shape a lasting legacy for your family and loved ones.

Building wealth is not just about achieving financial security during our lifetime; it's also about creating a foundation for the prosperity of those who come after us. In this chapter, we'll explore various aspects of legacy planning, from understanding the significance of leaving a legacy to practical steps for transferring wealth efficiently.

Legacy planning involves more than just financial assets; it encompasses your values, beliefs, and the impact you want to have on the lives of those you care about. We'll delve into the process of articulating and documenting your values, ensuring that your legacy aligns with your personal principles and goals.

Efficient wealth transfer involves navigating the complexities of estate planning, wills, and trusts. We'll guide you through these legal aspects, breaking down the jargon and providing insights into how you can structure your assets to minimize tax implications and ensure a seamless transfer of wealth.

Moreover, this chapter will emphasize the importance of communication within families about financial matters and estate plans. Open and honest conversations can foster understanding, mitigate potential conflicts, and ensure that everyone involved is on the same page regarding your legacy intentions.

As we explore the multifaceted dimensions of legacy and wealth transfer, keep in mind that building a legacy is a dynamic and ongoing process. Whether you're just beginning to consider these aspects or have existing plans in place, this chapter aims to provide valuable insights and actionable steps to help you shape a meaningful and enduring legacy for generations to come.

Securing Your Legacy

Ensuring a lasting legacy is a profound endeavor that transcends financial considerations. Chapter 13, Section 13.1, delves into the intricacies of securing your legacy—a legacy that encapsulates not only your material wealth but also the values, principles, and impact you wish to imprint on the world.

At its core, securing your legacy involves a holistic approach that goes beyond the legalities of estate planning. It begins with a deep introspection into what matters most to you. What values define your life, and how do you want those values to endure through the generations that follow?

One crucial aspect of securing your legacy is articulating your values and beliefs. Take the time to document what matters to you, what you stand for, and the principles that have guided your life. This not only provides clarity for you but also serves as a guiding light for your heirs, helping them understand the ethos that underpins your legacy.

Estate planning is a pivotal component of securing your legacy, encompassing wills, trusts, and other legal instruments. It's essential to work with legal professionals who specialize in estate law to ensure that your wishes are clearly outlined and legally sound. This process involves considering not only the distribution of financial assets but also personal belongings, real estate, and any sentimental items that hold significant value.

Moreover, taxes are an inevitable aspect of wealth transfer, and understanding how they impact your estate is crucial. Knowledgeable financial advisors can help you navigate tax implications, implementing strategies to minimize the burden on your heirs.

Another critical dimension of legacy security is fostering open communication within your family. Discussing your estate plans, values, and intentions can prevent misunderstandings and potential conflicts down the road. Family meetings, guided by transparency and honesty, can provide clarity and ensure that everyone involved comprehends and respects your legacy goals.

Beyond financial assets, consider the impact you want to have on the community and causes that matter to you. Charitable giving and philanthropy can be integral components of your legacy, leaving a positive imprint on the world.

In essence, securing your legacy is an ongoing process that requires thoughtful consideration, legal expertise, and open communication. By approaching it holistically, considering both tangible and intangible elements, you can create a legacy that not only endures through material wealth but also resonates with the values that define your life.

ESTATE PLANNING FOR MOMS

Estate planning is a significant undertaking for moms, as it involves not just the distribution of financial assets but also the well-being and future security of their families. In Section 13.1.1, we explore the nuances of estate planning tailored specifically for mothers, recognizing the unique roles and responsibilities they hold.

One of the primary considerations in estate planning for moms is the guardianship of minor children. Naming a legal guardian ensures that, in the unfortunate event of a mother's passing, there's a designated individual who will take responsibility for the children's upbringing. This decision involves thoughtful consideration of the guardian's values, parenting style, and ability to provide emotional and financial support.

Wills and trusts play a pivotal role in estate planning for moms. These legal instruments allow mothers to outline how their assets should be distributed, ensuring that their children and other beneficiaries receive the intended financial support. Trusts, in particular, can provide a structured approach to managing and distributing assets over time, offering financial protection for the family.

Life insurance is another crucial aspect. For moms, having adequate life insurance coverage is essential to provide a financial safety net for their families. The proceeds from a life insurance policy can help cover ongoing living expenses, mortgage payments, and children's education costs.

Considering the potential tax implications of estate planning is also vital. Working with financial advisors who specialize in estate law can help moms navigate tax considerations, ensuring that the transfer of assets is as efficient and tax-friendly as possible.

In the context of blended families, estate planning becomes even more intricate. Moms with stepchildren may need to navigate complex family dynamics and ensure that their wishes align with the legal obligations and rights of all family members.

Estate planning for moms extends beyond financial considerations to include personal belongings and sentimental items. Clearly articulating the distribution of these items in a will can prevent disputes and ensure that cherished possessions find their way to the intended recipients.

Regularly reviewing and updating the estate plan is essential, especially in the face of life changes such as births, deaths, marriages, or divorces. Staying proactive in this regard helps moms adapt their plans to evolving circumstances, ensuring that the estate plan remains aligned with their wishes and the best interests of their families.

In essence, estate planning for moms is a comprehensive process that requires careful consideration of family dynamics, financial obligations, and the desire to leave a lasting legacy. By addressing these aspects thoughtfully, moms can create a robust estate plan that provides for their families and aligns with their values and intentions.

TEACHING FINANCIAL RESPONSIBILITY TO FUTURE GENERATIONS

Passing on financial wisdom to future generations is a gift that lasts a lifetime. In this section, we delve into the importance of teaching financial responsibility to children and grandchildren as part of securing your legacy.

Parents often aspire to equip their children with the skills to navigate the financial landscape independently. Teaching financial responsibility isn't just about dollars and cents; it's about instilling values, habits, and a mindset that will serve the next generation well.

Start early in imparting financial education. Introducing basic concepts like saving, budgeting, and the value of money can begin in childhood. Engaging children in age-appropriate discussions about money fosters a healthy understanding of its role in their lives.

Lead by example. Children are observant, and they often learn more from what they see than what they're told. Demonstrating responsible financial behaviors, such as budgeting, saving, and making informed spending decisions, provides a powerful model for them to emulate.

Encourage a hands-on approach to money management. Allowing children to manage a small allowance or earnings from chores can be an effective way for them to learn about budgeting and making choices with their money. These practical experiences lay the foundation for responsible financial habits.

Incorporate financial lessons into everyday life. From grocery shopping to planning family outings, there are numerous opportunities to discuss money matters. By integrating financial conversations into daily activities, parents can help demystify financial concepts and make them a natural part of family discussions.

Teach the value of delayed gratification. In an era of instant gratification, instilling the ability to wait for rewards and save for future goals is a crucial lesson. This skill is fundamental not only for financial success but also for personal and professional growth.

Introduce the concept of investing. As children grow older, introducing them to the basics of investing can be valuable. Explaining how investments work, the concept of risk and return, and the potential benefits of long-term investing can empower them to make informed financial decisions.

Foster an open dialogue about money. Creating a safe space for discussing financial matters without judgment encourages children to ask questions, seek guidance, and share their own thoughts about money. This open dialogue lays the groundwork for a healthy relationship with finances.

Extend financial education beyond the immediate family. Collaborating with schools, community programs, or online resources can supplement the financial education provided at home. Encouraging a love for learning about money and finances can set the stage for a lifetime of financial literacy.

Ultimately, teaching financial responsibility to future generations is an ongoing process that evolves as children grow and their financial needs and challenges change. By instilling strong financial values and habits early on, moms can contribute to the financial well-being and success of their children and future generations.

Wealth Transfer Strategies

Wealth transfer strategies are a crucial aspect of securing your legacy and ensuring that the financial well-being of your loved ones is preserved for generations to come. This section explores various approaches to wealth transfer, emphasizing the importance of thoughtful planning and careful consideration.

One of the fundamental components of wealth transfer is estate planning. Crafting a comprehensive estate plan involves detailing how your assets will be distributed upon your passing. This includes wills, trusts, and other legal instruments that can help minimize tax implications and streamline the transfer of assets.

Trusts are powerful tools in wealth transfer planning. They allow you to set aside assets for specific purposes or beneficiaries, providing a level of control and protection that might not be achievable through a simple will. Trusts can be tailored to meet unique family circumstances, such as providing for minors, individuals with special needs, or ensuring the orderly transition of family businesses.

Gifting is another strategy that enables you to transfer wealth while you are still alive. By gifting assets, whether in the form of cash, property, or investments, you can potentially reduce the size of your taxable estate. It also provides you with the gratification of witnessing the impact of your generosity during your lifetime.

Strategic life insurance planning can be instrumental in wealth transfer. Life insurance policies can provide a tax-efficient means of passing on wealth to beneficiaries. The death benefit from a life insurance policy is generally income-tax-free and can be a valuable source of liquidity for covering estate taxes or equalizing inheritances among heirs.

Consideration of tax implications is integral to effective wealth transfer. Estate taxes, gift taxes, and generation-skipping transfer taxes are all factors that need to be assessed and managed. Leveraging available exemptions, deductions, and credits can help minimize the tax burden on your estate and maximize the assets available for transfer.

Engaging in open communication with your heirs about your wealth transfer plan is crucial. Transparent discussions about your intentions, the values underpinning your decisions, and any conditions associated with inheritances can help prevent misunderstandings and foster a sense of responsibility among beneficiaries.

Charitable giving is a meaningful aspect of wealth transfer. Establishing a family foundation or contributing to charitable causes can be a way to leave a lasting legacy while potentially enjoying tax benefits. It also instills a sense of philanthropy in future generations.

Regularly reviewing and updating your wealth transfer plan is essential. Life circumstances, tax laws, and financial markets can change, necessitating adjustments to ensure your plan remains aligned with your goals and objectives.

In conclusion, wealth transfer strategies involve a combination of legal, financial, and interpersonal considerations. By taking a holistic approach to planning, moms can create a roadmap that not only preserves their financial legacy but also nurtures the well-being and prosperity of their descendants.

GIFTING AND INHERITANCE PLANNING

Gifting and inheritance planning play pivotal roles in the broader spectrum of wealth transfer strategies, offering unique opportunities to mold the financial legacy you leave for your loved ones. This section delves into the intricacies of gifting and inheritance planning, shedding light on the nuances that can significantly impact the smooth transition of assets from one generation to the next.

Gifting during your lifetime is a proactive strategy that allows you to share your wealth with heirs while potentially reducing the size of your taxable estate. By making strategic gifts, you not only provide financial support to your loved ones but also have the satisfaction of witnessing the positive impact of your generosity. It's important to be mindful of the annual gift tax exclusion, which allows you to gift a certain amount to each recipient without triggering gift taxes.

Furthermore, gifting can extend beyond straightforward transfers of cash. You can gift appreciated assets, such as stocks or real estate, taking advantage of potential tax benefits. This can be a strategic way to divest yourself of certain assets while aligning with your overall financial goals and minimizing the tax burden for your heirs.

Inheritance planning, on the other hand, involves the systematic distribution of assets upon your passing. A carefully crafted estate plan, which may include wills and trusts, ensures that your wishes regarding asset distribution are honored. Trusts, in particular, offer a level of control over how and when heirs receive their inheritances, providing flexibility to address unique family circumstances.

Consideration of the emotional and financial preparedness of heirs is integral to effective gifting and inheritance planning. Engaging in open and transparent communication with family members can help manage expectations, prevent potential conflicts, and foster a sense of responsibility among beneficiaries. Clearly articulating your intentions, values, and any conditions associated with inheritances contributes to a harmonious transition.

Incorporating charitable giving into your gifting and inheritance plan adds a philanthropic dimension to your legacy. Establishing a family foundation or incorporating charitable bequests in your will allows you to contribute to causes that align with your values. It also introduces the concept of social responsibility to heirs, encouraging a legacy of giving back to the community.

Professional guidance from estate planning attorneys and financial advisors can be instrumental in navigating the complexities of gifting and inheritance planning. They can help structure your plan in a tax-efficient manner, ensuring that your assets are distributed in accordance with your wishes while minimizing the impact of estate and gift taxes.

Regular reviews and updates to your gifting and inheritance plan are crucial to account for changes in family dynamics, tax laws, and financial circumstances. By taking a proactive and comprehensive approach to these strategies, you can create a lasting financial legacy that reflects your values and supports the well-being of future generations.

ENSURING FINANCIAL STABILITY FOR HEIRS

Ensuring financial stability for heirs is a crucial aspect of comprehensive wealth transfer planning. This section explores the various considerations and strategies involved in safeguarding the financial well-being of your loved ones after your passing, emphasizing the importance of foresight, proper planning, and ongoing communication.

One of the primary pillars of financial stability for heirs is education. Providing heirs with financial literacy and education equips them with the knowledge and skills needed to manage their inheritances responsibly. This education can encompass basic financial principles, investment strategies, and the potential tax implications associated with inherited assets.

Incorporating trusts into your estate plan can be a powerful tool for ensuring the financial stability of heirs. Trusts offer the flexibility to dictate how, when, and under what conditions heirs receive their inheritances. This can be particularly beneficial if you have concerns about heirs' financial management capabilities, are dealing with minor beneficiaries, or wish to protect assets from creditors.

Considering the unique needs and circumstances of each heir is essential. While equal distribution may seem fair on the surface, it might not be equitable in all cases. Factors such as individual financial situations, career paths, and personal responsibilities should be taken into account when designing an inheritance plan. This personalized approach ensures that each heir receives the support necessary for their specific circumstances.

Life insurance can also play a vital role in ensuring financial stability for heirs. By designating heirs as beneficiaries, life insurance policies can provide a tax-free influx of funds upon your passing. This can be especially valuable for covering immediate expenses, such as funeral costs, estate taxes, or outstanding debts, without the need to liquidate other assets.

Communication is key to the success of any wealth transfer plan. Discussing your intentions and the reasoning behind your decisions with heirs fosters understanding and minimizes the potential for disputes. It also allows heirs to prepare for their financial futures, aligning their expectations with the reality of their inheritances.

In the context of financial stability, ongoing communication extends beyond your passing. If you foresee the need for continued financial support, such as for education, homeownership, or starting a business, outlining these expectations in your estate plan ensures that your wishes are carried out effectively.

Encouraging heirs to seek professional financial advice is another proactive measure. This guidance can help them make informed decisions regarding investments, tax planning, and overall financial management. By promoting financial literacy and providing access to resources, you empower heirs to navigate the complexities of managing inherited wealth responsibly.

Regularly reviewing and updating your estate plan is essential to adapt to changing circumstances and ensure that it remains aligned with your intentions. Life events, such as marriages, births, or changes in financial status, may necessitate adjustments to your wealth transfer strategy.

In essence, ensuring financial stability for heirs involves a thoughtful and personalized approach that encompasses education, strategic planning, and open communication. By addressing the unique needs and circumstances of each heir, you contribute to the creation of a lasting financial legacy that enhances the well-being of your loved ones for generations to come.

Chapter 14: Sustainable Financial Habits

Welcome to Chapter 14, where we delve into the realm of sustainable financial habits. In the journey toward financial well-being, sustainability goes beyond mere stability; it involves cultivating habits that promote long-term health and resilience for your finances. This chapter explores practices and mindsets that not only sustain your financial health today but also lay the groundwork for a secure and flourishing future.

Think of sustainable financial habits as the daily nourishment that fuels your financial resilience. These habits encompass a wide array of practices, from mindful spending and savings strategies to ethical investing and eco-conscious financial decisions. The goal is to create a financial ecosystem that thrives and adapts over time, ensuring that your resources align with your values and contribute to a better world.

As we navigate through this chapter, you'll discover practical insights and actionable steps to integrate sustainability into your financial habits. Whether you're aiming to reduce your ecological footprint, make socially responsible investment choices, or simply create a financial legacy aligned with your values, this chapter serves as your guide.

The concept of sustainability extends beyond the environmental sphere to encompass financial mindfulness and responsibility. It's about making choices today that don't compromise the well-being of your future self or the generations that follow. From budgeting techniques that stand the test of time to investment strategies that consider long-term impacts, sustainable financial habits provide the framework for enduring financial success.

Throughout these pages, we'll explore how small, consistent actions can lead to significant positive changes. By weaving sustainability into your financial fabric, you'll not only secure your own financial future but also contribute to the greater good. So, let's embark on this journey together, discovering the joy and fulfillment that comes from building a financial life that stands strong, adapts to change, and leaves a positive mark on the world. Welcome to the world of sustainable financial habits!

Developing Sustainable Money Habits

Embarking on the journey of developing sustainable money habits involves fostering a mindset that prioritizes long-term financial health and responsible decision-making. At its core, sustainability in the realm of personal finance means making choices today that not only benefit your current financial well-being but also set the stage for enduring prosperity.

Central to this concept is the understanding that every financial decision, no matter how small, carries the potential for long-lasting impact. Sustainable money habits are akin to planting seeds that, with time and nurturing, grow into sturdy trees providing shade and sustenance. It's about recognizing the interconnectedness of your financial choices and their collective influence on your financial ecosystem.

One key aspect of sustainable money habits is mindful spending. This involves cultivating an awareness of your financial inflows and outflows, understanding the value of your purchases, and making intentional decisions that align with your financial goals. Rather than succumbing to impulsive spending, consider the long-term implications of your choices and how they contribute to your overall financial landscape.

Savings also play a crucial role in sustainability. Developing a habit of consistent and purposeful saving ensures that you're building a financial cushion for unforeseen circumstances and future goals. It's not just about saving for the sake of it; it's about creating a resilient financial foundation that can weather storms and support your aspirations.

Moreover, sustainable money habits extend beyond personal gain to encompass the broader impact of your financial decisions. Ethical considerations in spending and investing become integral components. This involves supporting businesses and initiatives that align with your values, as well as making investment choices that contribute to positive social and environmental outcomes.

Another dimension of sustainability in personal finance is adaptability. Just as ecosystems evolve and adapt to changes, your financial habits should demonstrate flexibility in response to shifts in your life circumstances. This might involve adjusting your budget, reevaluating financial goals, or exploring new investment opportunities.

In essence, developing sustainable money habits is a holistic approach to personal finance. It's a mindset that values the longevity of your financial well-being, embraces conscious decision-making, and recognizes the ripple effects of each choice. As you cultivate these habits, you're not only securing your own financial future but also contributing to the broader goal of creating a sustainable and thriving financial ecosystem for yourself and those who come after you.

CONSISTENCY IN BUDGETING AND SAVING

Consistency in budgeting and saving forms the bedrock of sustainable financial habits, echoing the proverbial wisdom that "little drops of water make a mighty ocean." This section delves into the profound impact that the steadfast commitment to budgeting and saving can have on your financial well-being, fostering resilience and paving the way for long-term prosperity.

At its essence, budgeting is a dynamic and ongoing process rather than a one-time event. It involves conscientiously allocating your financial resources to various aspects of your life, aligning your spending with your priorities, and ensuring that you're saving for both short-term needs and future goals. Consistency in this practice is like tending to a garden; regular care and attention yield a flourishing landscape.

When you consistently adhere to a well-thought-out budget, you gain a comprehensive understanding of your financial inflows and outflows. This awareness empowers you to make informed decisions, avoid unnecessary debt, and channel your resources toward endeavors that truly matter to you. By cultivating the habit of intentional budgeting, you create a financial roadmap that guides you through various life stages, adapting as your circumstances evolve.

Savings, the faithful companion of budgeting, adds a layer of financial security and opportunity. Consistently saving a portion of your income, whether it's for emergencies, future investments, or retirement, establishes a financial safety net. This safety net not only shields you from unexpected financial shocks but also provides you with the means to pursue your goals with confidence.

Moreover, the consistency in saving cultivates discipline and resilience. It reinforces the principle of delayed gratification, encouraging you to look beyond immediate desires and prioritize long-term financial health. This habit is particularly powerful when faced with the myriad temptations of consumer culture, as it instills the mindset that sustainable financial well-being is a marathon, not a sprint.

Consistency in budgeting and saving is not about rigidly adhering to a fixed set of rules. Rather, it involves adapting your financial habits to suit your lifestyle and goals while maintaining a core commitment to financial responsibility. Life is dynamic, and so should be your approach to budgeting and saving.

In the realm of personal finance, consistency breeds confidence. It builds a foundation of financial stability that withstands the ebb and flow of life's uncertainties. As you consistently allocate resources toward your priorities and diligently save for the future, you not only enhance your own financial well-being but also contribute to the broader sustainability of your financial ecosystem. This section underscores the transformative power of steadfast commitment to budgeting and saving, emphasizing how these habits can turn your financial aspirations into tangible realities.

ADJUSTING FINANCIAL HABITS OVER TIME

Adjusting financial habits over time is a natural and essential aspect of personal financial management. Life is dynamic, and your financial landscape evolves with it. This section explores the importance of adaptability in financial habits, emphasizing the need to recalibrate strategies as you navigate through different life stages and circumstances.

One of the fundamental truths in personal finance is that change is constant. What worked for you in your 20s may not be as suitable in your 40s, and what was once a financial priority may shift as your family grows or your career takes new directions. Acknowledging and embracing these changes is the first step toward financial resilience and success.

Life events such as marriage, the birth of a child, or a career shift can significantly impact your financial priorities and obligations. As these milestones unfold, it's crucial to reassess your financial habits. For instance, you may need to reallocate resources to accommodate new family needs or adjust your budget to reflect changes in income and expenses. Flexibility is key to ensuring that your financial habits remain aligned with your evolving goals.

Similarly, economic conditions and external factors can influence your financial landscape. A recession, for instance, may necessitate a more conservative approach to investment, while a period of economic growth could present opportunities for strategic financial moves. Being attuned to the broader economic environment allows you to make informed adjustments to your financial habits, ensuring they remain relevant and effective.

Moreover, personal growth and development play a pivotal role in financial well-being. As you advance in your career, acquire new skills, or explore entrepreneurial endeavors, your financial habits should evolve to accommodate these changes. This might involve revisiting your budget to allocate resources for professional development, adjusting your savings strategy to align with new income levels, or exploring investment opportunities that align with your expanded financial goals.

Adjusting financial habits over time is not an admission of failure; rather, it's a demonstration of wisdom and adaptability. It reflects your commitment to staying attuned to your financial reality and making intentional choices that serve your best interests. By periodically evaluating and adjusting your financial habits, you position yourself to navigate the complexities of life with resilience and confidence.

In essence, the ability to adapt your financial habits over time is a superpower in personal finance. It allows you to weather life's storms, seize emerging opportunities, and stay aligned with your evolving aspirations. This section encourages readers to embrace the dynamic nature of personal finance, offering insights into the art of adjusting financial habits as a means of fostering long-term financial success and well-being.

Staying Motivated on the Financial Freedom Journey

Embarking on the journey toward financial freedom is akin to a marathon rather than a sprint. It's a long-term commitment that requires dedication, resilience, and, most importantly, sustained motivation. In this section, we delve into the strategies and mindset shifts that can help individuals stay motivated on their financial freedom journey.

The path to financial freedom is often dotted with challenges, setbacks, and unexpected turns. It's not uncommon to encounter moments of doubt or frustration, especially when faced with unexpected expenses, market fluctuations, or personal setbacks. Therefore, cultivating and maintaining motivation is crucial to staying on course.

One of the primary motivators on the financial freedom journey is having a clear vision of your goals. Whether it's retiring early, buying a home, or funding your children's education, having a vivid mental picture of what financial freedom means to you provides a tangible target to strive toward. This vision acts as a North Star, guiding your financial decisions and helping you navigate the inevitable ups and downs.

Additionally, breaking down larger financial goals into smaller, manageable milestones can make the journey more achievable and less overwhelming. Celebrating these small wins along the way provides a sense of accomplishment and reinforces the idea that progress is being made. It's essential to acknowledge and appreciate the effort invested in reaching each milestone, reinforcing the positive habits that contribute to financial success.

Another powerful motivator is understanding the "why" behind your financial goals. Beyond the surface-level objectives, dig deeper to uncover the emotional and personal reasons driving your pursuit of financial freedom. Whether it's providing security for your family, pursuing passions, or contributing to causes you care about, connecting your financial goals to your values adds a profound layer of motivation.

Moreover, staying engaged and informed about personal finance can help sustain motivation. This doesn't mean obsessively tracking every market movement but rather developing a basic understanding of financial principles, investment strategies, and economic trends. Knowledge empowers individuals to make informed decisions and builds confidence in their financial journey.

Surrounding yourself with a supportive community can also be a potent motivator. Share your financial goals with friends, family, or like-minded individuals who can provide encouragement, advice, and accountability. Knowing that you're not alone in your journey fosters a sense of camaraderie and reinforces the shared pursuit of financial well-being.

Lastly, embracing a positive mindset is foundational to maintaining motivation. Recognize that setbacks are a natural part of any journey, and use them as opportunities to learn and adjust course if needed. Practice self-compassion, celebrate progress, and approach challenges with a solution-oriented mindset.

In conclusion, staying motivated on the financial freedom journey requires a combination of vision, goal-setting, self-reflection, knowledge, community support, and a positive mindset. By integrating these elements into your approach, you can navigate the complexities of personal finance with resilience, focus, and unwavering motivation. This section aims to inspire and guide readers on cultivating the mindset necessary for long-term financial success.

CELEBRATING FINANCIAL MILESTONES

Amidst the journey towards financial freedom, it's crucial to pause and celebrate the milestones achieved along the way. These financial milestones are not just markers of progress; they're victories that deserve recognition and reflection. In this section, we explore the importance of celebrating financial milestones and how this practice can enhance the overall experience of the financial freedom journey.

Financial milestones come in various forms, whether it's paying off a significant portion of debt, reaching a certain savings threshold, or achieving a specific investment goal. These accomplishments represent the tangible outcomes of hard work, discipline, and strategic decision-making. By taking the time to acknowledge and celebrate these milestones, individuals can cultivate a positive and empowering relationship with their financial journey.

Celebrating financial milestones is not merely about indulging in a momentary sense of achievement. It serves a more profound purpose by reinforcing positive financial behaviors. When individuals recognize their progress and the positive impact of their financial decisions, they are more likely to stay motivated and committed to their long-term goals.

Moreover, the act of celebration creates a positive association with financial success. It transforms what might feel like a challenging and arduous journey into a series of triumphs. This positive reinforcement builds confidence, fosters a sense of accomplishment, and propels individuals forward with renewed enthusiasm.

Celebration doesn't necessarily mean extravagant gestures or expensive treats. It can be as simple as reflecting on the journey, expressing gratitude for the achievements, or treating oneself to a small, meaningful reward. The key is to make the celebration proportionate to the significance of the milestone, creating a balance between acknowledgment and maintaining financial discipline.

The celebration of financial milestones is also an opportune time for self-reflection. It provides individuals with the chance to assess what worked well in their financial strategy, understand the challenges faced, and identify lessons learned. This reflective practice contributes to ongoing financial growth by informing future decisions and refining financial plans.

Furthermore, sharing financial milestones with a supportive community, whether it's friends, family, or an online network, amplifies the joy and enhances the sense of achievement. The encouragement and positive feedback from others contribute to a shared celebration, fostering a sense of camaraderie on the financial freedom journey.

In conclusion, celebrating financial milestones is a pivotal aspect of the journey toward financial freedom. It transforms the process from a mere accumulation of wealth to a meaningful and empowering narrative of progress. By embracing the practice of celebration, individuals can infuse their financial journey with positivity, motivation, and a greater sense of purpose. This section aims to inspire readers to not only reach their financial milestones but to take the time to revel in the accomplishments, both big and small, along the way.

OVERCOMING SETBACKS AND CHALLENGES

Navigating the path to financial freedom is a journey filled with highs and lows, victories and challenges. In this section, we explore the inevitability of setbacks and challenges on the road to financial well-being and delve into the strategies and mindset needed to overcome them.

Setbacks are a natural part of any journey, and the financial freedom journey is no exception. Unexpected expenses, economic downturns, or personal circumstances can disrupt even the most carefully crafted financial plans. Acknowledging and understanding that setbacks are part of the process is the first step in overcoming them.

One of the key strategies for overcoming setbacks is resilience. Resilience involves the ability to adapt to challenges, bounce back from setbacks, and continue moving forward. Resilient individuals view setbacks as temporary obstacles rather than insurmountable roadblocks. They understand that setbacks are opportunities for growth and learning.

When faced with financial setbacks, it's essential to take a proactive and solution-oriented approach. Rather than dwelling on the challenges, focus on identifying potential solutions. This might involve reassessing your budget, exploring new income streams, or seeking professional advice. The key is to maintain a forward-looking mindset and take constructive steps to address the situation.

A strong support system plays a crucial role in overcoming financial challenges. Whether it's friends, family, or financial advisors, sharing your concerns and seeking advice can provide valuable perspectives and potential solutions. This collaborative approach not only eases the burden but also opens up new possibilities for overcoming challenges.

Mindset matters significantly when dealing with setbacks. Adopting a growth mindset, which sees challenges as opportunities for learning and improvement, can be transformative. Instead of viewing setbacks as failures, see them as feedback that guides you toward better financial decisions and strategies. This mindset shift fosters a positive outlook and encourages perseverance.

Flexibility is another key factor in overcoming setbacks. Financial plans are not rigid and should be adaptable to changing circumstances. Being flexible in your approach allows you to adjust your strategies when needed and navigate unexpected challenges more effectively. It's the ability to pivot without losing sight of your long-term goals.

In addition to resilience, proactive problem-solving, a strong support system, and a growth mindset, self-compassion is crucial when overcoming setbacks. Understand that everyone faces challenges, and setbacks do not define your financial journey. Treat yourself with kindness, learn from the experience, and use it as a stepping stone for future success.

Ultimately, setbacks are not roadblocks but detours on the path to financial freedom. By cultivating resilience, adopting a proactive mindset, seeking support, staying flexible, and practicing self-compassion, individuals can overcome challenges and continue progressing toward their financial goals. This section aims to inspire readers to embrace setbacks as opportunities for growth and develop the resilience needed to navigate the twists and turns on their journey to financial well-being.

Chapter 15: Health and Wellness

Welcome to Chapter 15 of our financial well-being guide, where we shift our focus to an equally vital aspect of a balanced and fulfilling life: health and wellness. Achieving financial freedom is a holistic journey that extends beyond monetary considerations, recognizing the profound impact that well-being has on our overall quality of life.

In this chapter, we explore the intricate connection between health and financial well-being. Health is an invaluable asset, and its significance cannot be overstated in the pursuit of a fulfilling life. As we delve into this intersection, we aim to provide insights, strategies, and considerations that empower you to make informed decisions regarding your health and, by extension, your financial stability.

Understanding the symbiotic relationship between health and finances is pivotal. A healthy lifestyle contributes not only to physical and mental well-being but also to long-term financial sustainability. Conversely, financial stability can provide the means to invest in your health, creating a positive feedback loop that enhances your overall quality of life.

This chapter will guide you through various aspects of health and wellness, offering practical tips on how to maintain a healthy lifestyle without straining your budget. We'll explore the importance of preventive care, mindful spending on healthcare, and strategies for balancing the pursuit of both financial and physical well-being.

As you navigate the pages of this chapter, remember that health is an ongoing journey rather than a destination. Small, consistent steps can lead to significant improvements in both your well-being and financial stability. By recognizing the interconnectedness of health and financial goals, you'll be better equipped to make informed choices that contribute to a more balanced and rewarding life.

Join us on this exploration of health and wellness, where we integrate practical financial wisdom with insights into nurturing your physical and mental well-being. Through a harmonious approach to health and finances, you can build a foundation for a prosperous and fulfilling life.

The Connection Between Financial and Physical Health

The interplay between financial health and physical well-being is a dynamic and intricate relationship that significantly impacts our overall quality of life. In this section, we'll delve into the profound connection between these two aspects and explore how nurturing one can positively influence the other.

Financial stability provides a robust foundation for maintaining physical health. When individuals have the means to access nutritious food, engage in regular exercise, and afford preventive healthcare, they are better positioned to lead a healthier lifestyle. Adequate financial resources contribute to stress reduction, enabling individuals to focus on self-care and preventive measures.

Conversely, physical health is a valuable asset that directly affects our financial situation. A healthy lifestyle often translates to lower healthcare costs in the long run. Regular exercise, a balanced diet, and preventive healthcare measures can mitigate the risk of chronic illnesses, reducing the financial burden associated with medical expenses. This creates a positive feedback loop where investments in health lead to financial savings.

Mental well-being, closely linked to both physical health and financial stability, further exemplifies this connection. Financial stress can take a toll on mental health, leading to anxiety and other psychological challenges. On the flip side, mental well-being influences our ability to make sound financial decisions. Emotional resilience and clarity of mind contribute to better financial planning and goal setting.

Understanding the link between financial and physical health empowers individuals to make informed choices. It encourages a holistic approach to well-being that goes beyond traditional boundaries. Recognizing the symbiotic relationship between these aspects allows for the creation of integrated strategies that address both financial and health goals simultaneously.

It's essential to acknowledge that the journey to optimal health and financial well-being is unique for each individual. Cultivating mindfulness around spending habits, prioritizing preventive healthcare, and adopting sustainable lifestyle choices are all pivotal components of this journey. Small, consistent efforts in these areas contribute to a resilient and harmonious balance between financial and physical health.

In conclusion, the connection between financial and physical health is undeniable. By recognizing and respecting this relationship, individuals can embark on a journey towards holistic well-being. The synergy between these two facets creates a roadmap for a fulfilling and prosperous life, where financial stability and physical health mutually reinforce each other, fostering resilience and vitality.

MANAGING STRESS FOR BETTER FINANCIAL DECISIONS

Navigating stress is an integral aspect of managing one's financial decisions and overall well-being. In this section, we'll explore the profound impact that stress can have on financial choices and how adopting effective stress management strategies can lead to better financial outcomes.

Stress, whether stemming from financial concerns or other life pressures, has the potential to significantly influence decision-making processes. When individuals experience stress, the brain's cognitive functions may be compromised, affecting reasoning, problem-solving, and long-term planning. In the context of financial decisions, this can lead to impulsive choices, increased risk-taking, and a diminished capacity for considering future consequences.

Understanding the relationship between stress and financial decision-making is crucial for building resilience. Financial stress, often triggered by concerns about debt, income instability, or unexpected expenses, can create a cycle of anxiety that permeates various aspects of life. This can lead to decisions driven by short-term relief rather than long-term financial well-being.

Effective stress management is not only beneficial for mental and physical health but also plays a pivotal role in fostering better financial decisions. Adopting mindfulness practices, such as meditation or deep breathing exercises, can help individuals develop emotional resilience. These practices enable individuals to approach financial decisions with a clearer and more composed mindset, mitigating the impact of stress on the decision-making process.

Financial education and planning also serve as powerful tools in stress management. When individuals have a comprehensive understanding of their financial situation and a well-defined plan for achieving their goals, it can alleviate some of the uncertainty that often contributes to stress. Creating a realistic budget, establishing an emergency fund, and setting achievable financial goals are practical steps in this direction.

Furthermore, seeking support from friends, family, or financial advisors can be instrumental in managing stress. Sharing concerns and collaborating on potential solutions not only provides emotional relief but also opens up opportunities for gaining valuable insights and advice.

It's essential to recognize that stress is a universal experience, and its impact on financial decisions is a shared challenge. By acknowledging stress as a natural response to life's uncertainties, individuals can reframe their relationship with stress. Rather than viewing it as an obstacle, they can see it as a signal for self-care and a prompt to employ effective stress management strategies.

In conclusion, managing stress is fundamental to making better financial decisions. By adopting mindfulness practices, enhancing financial literacy, and seeking support, individuals can break the cycle of stress-driven decision-making. This proactive approach not only improves financial outcomes but also contributes to overall well-being, creating a positive ripple effect in various facets of life.

15.1.2 AFFORDABLE HEALTH AND WELLNESS STRATEGIES

In this section, we'll delve into the importance of affordable health and wellness strategies, recognizing that maintaining well-being doesn't have to come with a hefty price tag. While it's true that some wellness practices may involve expenses, there are numerous affordable alternatives that contribute significantly to one's health and overall quality of life.

First and foremost, regular physical activity is a cornerstone of maintaining good health. Engaging in activities like walking, jogging, or home workouts requires minimal or no cost. Many communities also offer free or low-cost fitness classes, providing opportunities to stay active without breaking the bank. Physical wellness not only contributes to overall health but can also be a source of stress relief and mental well-being.

Nutrition plays a pivotal role in one's health, and adopting a balanced and nutritious diet need not be expensive. Planning meals in advance, opting for cost-effective yet nutritious foods like grains, legumes, and seasonal fruits and vegetables, and minimizing reliance on processed or convenience foods are practical steps in achieving affordable nutritional wellness.

Regular health check-ups and screenings are essential for preventive care. While healthcare costs can be a concern, many communities provide low-cost or free health clinics, ensuring access to basic medical services. Additionally, leveraging employer-sponsored wellness programs or community health events can be cost-effective ways to stay on top of one's health.

Mental health is an integral component of overall well-being, and there are various affordable strategies to support mental wellness. Practicing mindfulness and meditation, both of which can be learned through free online resources or community classes, are effective in managing stress and promoting mental clarity. Reading, journaling, and spending time in nature are simple yet impactful activities that contribute to mental well-being without significant financial investment.

When it comes to affordable wellness, adequate sleep should not be overlooked. Creating a conducive sleep environment and establishing a consistent sleep routine are budget-friendly practices that significantly impact overall health. Quality sleep is linked to improved cognitive function, emotional well-being, and physical health.

Community resources play a crucial role in making health and wellness affordable and accessible. Public parks, nature trails, and community centers often provide spaces for physical activities and recreational opportunities at little to no cost. Joining community-based groups focused on wellness, whether for exercise, nutrition, or mental health support, creates a sense of belonging and shared motivation.

In conclusion, prioritizing health and wellness does not require a significant financial investment. By incorporating affordable strategies like regular physical activity, balanced nutrition, preventive care through community clinics, and embracing mental health practices, individuals can cultivate a holistic approach to well-being. Affordable health and wellness are achievable through a combination of informed choices, community resources, and a commitment to maintaining a healthy lifestyle.

Balancing Self-Care with Financial Responsibility

In this section, we explore the delicate yet crucial balance between practicing self-care and maintaining financial responsibility. Striking the right equilibrium between caring for oneself and managing financial resources requires thoughtful consideration and intentional choices.

Self-care encompasses a broad spectrum of activities aimed at promoting physical, mental, and emotional well-being. From prioritizing quality sleep to engaging in activities that bring joy and relaxation, self-care is a personal journey. However, in the pursuit of self-care, it's essential to be mindful of the associated costs and ensure that these practices align with one's overall financial goals.

Financial responsibility involves making sound decisions to secure one's financial future. This includes budgeting, saving, investing wisely, and planning for unforeseen expenses. While these financial habits contribute to long-term stability, they should not come at the expense of neglecting self-care. The challenge lies in finding ways to nurture oneself without compromising fiscal responsibility.

One aspect of balancing self-care and financial responsibility is distinguishing between needs and wants. Identifying essential self-care practices that align with personal values can prevent unnecessary spending on fleeting indulgences. For instance, investing in quality sleep essentials, such as a comfortable mattress or blackout curtains, might be a wise expense compared to overspending on non-essential luxuries.

Similarly, embracing cost-effective self-care activities is pivotal. Enjoying a home-cooked meal, practicing meditation through free apps, or exploring outdoor activities can provide rejuvenation without straining the budget. This approach allows individuals to prioritize self-care without compromising financial stability.

Budgeting becomes a central tool in harmonizing self-care with financial responsibility. Allocating a portion of the budget to self-care allows for intentional spending on activities or products that contribute to well-being. By incorporating self-care into the budget, individuals can enjoy the benefits without the guilt associated with unplanned expenses.

Another consideration is exploring affordable alternatives for traditional self-care practices. Rather than expensive spa treatments, individuals can opt for at-home pampering sessions or seek community-based wellness programs that offer affordable services. Additionally, finding joy in simple pleasures, such as reading, spending time in nature, or connecting with loved ones, reinforces the idea that self-care need not be synonymous with extravagant spending.

In the pursuit of a balanced approach, it's essential to revisit and adjust priorities over time. Life circumstances, financial goals, and personal preferences evolve, requiring periodic reassessment of how self-care practices align with financial responsibility. Flexibility and adaptability are key to maintaining equilibrium on this journey.

In conclusion, balancing self-care with financial responsibility is an ongoing process that involves thoughtful decision-making and intentional choices. By identifying essential self-care practices, embracing cost-effective alternatives, integrating self-care into the budget, and remaining flexible in adjusting priorities, individuals can achieve harmony between nurturing themselves and safeguarding their financial well-being. The interplay between self-care and financial responsibility is dynamic, and a mindful approach ensures that both aspects contribute positively to an individual's overall quality of life.

PRIORITIZING MENTAL HEALTH

Prioritizing mental health is a fundamental aspect of overall well-being, and its significance cannot be overstated. In this section, we delve into the importance of making mental health a top priority, exploring the symbiotic relationship between mental well-being and financial stability.

Mental health encompasses emotional, psychological, and social well-being. It affects how individuals think, feel, and act, playing a pivotal role in shaping their ability to handle stress, relate to others, and make decisions. Prioritizing mental health involves recognizing its value and integrating practices that foster a positive mental state into one's daily life.

The connection between mental health and financial stability is intricate. Stress, anxiety, and other mental health challenges can significantly impact financial decision-making, potentially leading to impulsive choices, overspending, or neglecting financial responsibilities. Conversely, financial stress can exacerbate mental health issues, creating a cycle that can be challenging to break.

One key aspect of prioritizing mental health is fostering self-awareness. Understanding one's emotional and mental state allows for proactive measures to maintain balance. This involves recognizing stressors, triggers, and signs of mental health challenges. By acknowledging these factors, individuals can take preemptive steps to manage stress and protect their mental well-being.

Incorporating stress-reducing practices into daily life is a crucial component of prioritizing mental health. This can include mindfulness exercises, deep breathing techniques, or engaging in activities that bring joy and relaxation. The objective is to create a mental health toolkit tailored to individual needs, providing accessible resources for moments of stress or unease.

Building a support system is another vital element. Cultivating strong connections with friends, family, or mental health professionals provides a network of support during challenging times. Having open and honest conversations about mental health reduces stigma and encourages a culture of understanding and empathy.

Financial decisions impact mental health, and vice versa. Therefore, maintaining financial health contributes to a positive mental state. Establishing a clear financial plan, budgeting effectively, and saving for the future can reduce financial stressors. Moreover, seeking professional advice when needed can provide clarity and confidence in financial decision-making.

Employers and workplaces play a role in supporting mental health. Organizations fostering a culture of well-being, offering mental health resources, and providing flexibility can positively influence employees' mental health. Balancing work demands with mental health needs creates an environment where individuals feel supported in both their professional and personal lives.

Education also plays a crucial role in prioritizing mental health. Promoting awareness and understanding of mental health challenges reduces stigma and encourages early intervention. Financial literacy programs that address the intersection of mental health and financial well-being can empower individuals to make informed decisions.

In conclusion, prioritizing mental health is an ongoing commitment that requires self-awareness, proactive practices, and a supportive environment. The intricate link between mental well-being and financial stability emphasizes the need for a holistic approach. By recognizing the interplay between mental health and financial decisions, individuals can foster a positive mindset, make informed choices, and contribute to their overall wellness.

CREATING HEALTHY HABITS ON A BUDGET

Creating healthy habits on a budget is not only possible but also an essential aspect of maintaining overall well-being. In this section, we explore practical strategies for cultivating healthy habits that align with financial constraints, demonstrating that a healthy lifestyle is accessible to everyone.

When faced with budgetary constraints, it's crucial to approach health and wellness with a mindset of resourcefulness and creativity. Exercise, a cornerstone of a healthy lifestyle, doesn't have to involve expensive gym memberships or high-end equipment. Simple yet effective activities like walking, jogging, or practicing bodyweight exercises at home are budget-friendly alternatives. Utilizing free online resources, such as workout videos or fitness apps, can provide guidance and motivation without incurring additional costs.

Nutrition is another vital component of a healthy lifestyle. While there may be a perception that nutritious food is more expensive, strategic planning can make healthy eating affordable. Buying in bulk, opting for seasonal produce, and preparing meals at home are effective ways to stretch the budget. Additionally, exploring local farmers' markets or discount stores for fresh, affordable options can contribute to a balanced and budget-conscious diet.

Prioritizing mental health on a budget involves incorporating stress-relieving practices that don't strain finances. Mindfulness and meditation, for example, can be practiced without the need for expensive classes or equipment. Numerous free or low-cost apps and online resources provide guided meditation sessions, making this valuable practice accessible to all.

Adequate sleep is a fundamental aspect of overall well-being. Establishing a consistent sleep routine, optimizing sleep hygiene, and creating a comfortable sleep environment contribute to better sleep quality. These habits require minimal financial investment but yield significant health benefits.

Preventive healthcare is a key component of maintaining overall health. While healthcare costs can be a concern, seeking out affordable options, such as community health clinics or discounted services, can ensure that preventive measures are accessible. Taking advantage of free or low-cost health screenings and vaccinations is an effective strategy for managing health within budgetary constraints.

Social connections and community engagement are crucial for mental and emotional well-being. Engaging in social activities doesn't have to be expensive; attending community events, joining local clubs or groups, and participating in volunteer activities provide opportunities for connection without straining finances.

Balancing self-care with financial responsibility involves making intentional choices that align with one's budgetary constraints. It's about recognizing that well-being is multifaceted and can be nurtured through mindful choices that consider both physical and financial health. By adopting a holistic approach to health and wellness, individuals can create sustainable habits that support their overall well-being, regardless of their budget.

Chapter 16

Chapter 16: Long-Term Financial Planning

Welcome to Chapter 16: Long-Term Financial Planning, where we delve into the intricacies of securing your financial future. In this chapter, we explore the importance of thinking ahead and crafting a comprehensive plan that goes beyond day-to-day expenses. Long-term financial planning is not just about accumulating wealth; it's about ensuring financial security, peace of mind, and the ability to navigate life's uncertainties with confidence.

The journey towards financial stability is an ongoing process that requires foresight, strategic thinking, and adaptability. Whether you're just starting your career, raising a family, or approaching retirement, long-term financial planning is a dynamic and personalized endeavor. It involves setting realistic goals, making informed investment decisions, and preparing for the unexpected.

Throughout this chapter, we'll discuss various aspects of long-term financial planning, including retirement savings, investment strategies, legacy planning, and more. We'll provide insights into creating a roadmap that aligns with your aspirations and adapts to life's changing circumstances.

Planning for the future doesn't mean sacrificing the joys of the present. Instead, it empowers you to live a fulfilling life today while building a foundation for a secure and prosperous tomorrow. We'll explore how to strike a balance between enjoying the present and preparing for the future, making wise financial decisions that resonate with your values and lifestyle.

No matter where you are on your financial journey, it's never too early or too late to embark on long-term financial planning. The key is to approach it with intentionality, informed decision-making, and a commitment to continuous learning. So, let's dive into the world of long-term financial planning, where your goals become milestones, and your financial future becomes a well-crafted story of success and security.

Adjusting Financial Plans for Changing Circumstances

In the intricate tapestry of life, change is the only constant, and as we navigate the dynamic landscape of personal and economic circumstances, our financial plans must evolve alongside. Chapter 16, Section 16.2, sheds light on the art of Adjusting Financial Plans for Changing Circumstances—a crucial skill on the journey to long-term financial well-being.

Life is unpredictable, and unexpected events can have a significant impact on our financial landscapes. Whether it's a career shift, a family expansion, or unforeseen economic shifts, being able to adapt your financial plan is paramount. Embracing flexibility in your approach allows you to weather the storms and seize new opportunities that arise.

One of the cornerstones of adapting financial plans is the ability to reassess and reallocate resources. This involves regularly reviewing your budget, investments, and overall financial strategy to ensure they align with your current goals and circumstances. It's not about rigidly adhering to a pre-determined plan but rather about maintaining a dynamic relationship with your financial goals.

Career changes are a common catalyst for adjusting financial plans. Whether you're pursuing a new passion, switching industries, or starting a business, these shifts often come with financial implications. In this section, we explore how to navigate these transitions, including considerations like updating your budget, assessing the impact on savings and investments, and adjusting your long-term financial goals accordingly.

Family dynamics can also prompt adjustments to financial plans. Welcoming a new family member or dealing with unexpected changes in household size requires a reassessment of your budget, insurance coverage, and education savings. Flexibility in your financial plan enables you to accommodate these life-altering events seamlessly.

Economic fluctuations, both globally and locally, can impact your investments and income. Section 16.2 delves into strategies for navigating these uncertainties, emphasizing the importance of diversification, staying informed, and having a resilient mindset.

Additionally, this section explores the role of emergency funds in providing a financial safety net during unforeseen circumstances. Having a robust emergency fund is like having a financial cushion that can soften the impact of unexpected expenses or income disruptions, allowing you to make adjustments to your financial plan without compromising your stability.

Adapting financial plans for changing circumstances is not a sign of instability but rather a testament to financial wisdom. It's about embracing the ebb and flow of life, making intentional choices, and steering your financial ship with confidence. As we journey through this section, you'll discover the tools and mindset needed to adjust your financial sails and navigate the ever-changing seas of life.

DIVORCE AND FINANCIAL REASSESSMENT

Divorce is a profound life event that goes beyond emotional and relational aspects—it also has substantial financial implications. In Section 16.2.1, we explore the intricate terrain of Divorce and Financial Reassessment, recognizing the need for a thoughtful and strategic approach to navigating the complexities that arise during this transition.

When a marriage dissolves, financial arrangements that were once intertwined must now be carefully disentangled. The process can be emotionally challenging, but it necessitates a pragmatic examination of assets, liabilities, and financial goals. The goal is not just to survive financially but to thrive independently.

One crucial aspect is the division of assets and debts. This often involves assessing the value of shared properties, bank accounts, investments, and other assets acquired during the marriage. Financial experts, such as divorce attorneys and financial planners, can provide invaluable assistance in navigating this terrain, helping individuals make informed decisions about how to divide assets fairly.

Another consideration is alimony or spousal support. Section 16.2.1 delves into the factors that influence these arrangements, emphasizing the importance of understanding the financial implications for both parties involved. This section explores how individuals can plan for their financial future post-divorce, taking into account changes in income, expenses, and potential adjustments to lifestyle.

Additionally, the impact of divorce on long-term financial goals, such as retirement planning and children's education funds, is addressed. It underscores the need for reassessment and, if necessary, adjustment of these goals to reflect the new financial landscape.

Insurance coverage is another critical area that requires attention during and after divorce. From health insurance to life insurance and property coverage, Section 16.2.1 offers insights into ensuring that individuals maintain adequate protection for themselves and their dependents.

Importantly, this section also discusses the emotional toll of divorce and how seeking support, both from friends and family and potentially from professionals like therapists, can contribute to overall well-being during this challenging period.

Divorce is undoubtedly a major life transition, but with the right guidance and a proactive approach to financial reassessment, individuals can emerge from this experience with a solid foundation for their financial future. Section 16.2.1 serves as a guide, offering practical insights and strategies to empower individuals facing divorce to make sound financial decisions and pave the way for a new chapter in their lives.

PREPARING FOR UNEXPECTED LIFE EVENTS

Life is inherently unpredictable, and preparing for unexpected events is a cornerstone of responsible financial planning. In Section 16.2.2, we delve into the importance of Preparing for Unexpected Life Events, offering insights and strategies to fortify your financial resilience in the face of unforeseen circumstances.

Unforeseen life events can range from medical emergencies and accidents to sudden job loss or natural disasters. While it may be impossible to predict the exact nature of these events, being financially prepared can mitigate the impact and provide a sense of security during challenging times.

Firstly, Section 16.2.2 emphasizes the significance of building and maintaining an emergency fund. This financial cushion serves as a safety net, covering essential expenses like housing, utilities, and groceries in the event of an unforeseen crisis. The section provides guidance on determining the optimal size of your emergency fund based on your unique circumstances, ensuring that you're well-prepared for any unexpected turns life may take.

Insurance plays a pivotal role in safeguarding your financial well-being when the unexpected occurs. Health insurance, disability insurance, and life insurance are all explored in this section, shedding light on how these types of coverage can offer protection and financial support during challenging times. Understanding the terms and conditions of your policies, including any exclusions or limitations, is crucial for making informed decisions about the types and amounts of insurance coverage you need.

Beyond financial tools, Section 16.2.2 underscores the importance of having a comprehensive estate plan. This involves not only creating a will but also considering legal arrangements such as powers of attorney and healthcare directives. These documents ensure that your wishes are respected and that someone you trust can make decisions on your behalf if you're unable to do so.

Investing in your health is another key aspect of preparing for unexpected life events. Section 16.2.2 discusses the intersection of physical and financial well-being, emphasizing preventive measures and healthy lifestyle choices that can contribute to long-term resilience.

Lastly, this section addresses the psychological aspect of coping with unexpected events. Seeking emotional support, whether from friends, family, or mental health professionals, is highlighted as a crucial component of navigating challenges with resilience and positivity.

By proactively preparing for unexpected life events, you not only enhance your financial security but also cultivate a mindset of adaptability and strength. Section 16.2.2 serves as a guide, offering practical advice and empowering you to face life's uncertainties with confidence and resilience.

Chapter 17:
Celebrating Success

Welcome to Chapter 17: Celebrating Success – a chapter dedicated to acknowledging and reveling in the achievements along your financial journey. In the hustle and bustle of managing finances, it's easy to overlook the milestones, both big and small, that pave the way to financial well-being. This chapter encourages you to pause, reflect, and take pride in your accomplishments.

Financial success is a journey, not a destination, and recognizing the progress you've made is essential for maintaining motivation and sustaining positive financial habits. Whether you've paid off a significant debt, established an emergency fund, or achieved a savings goal, these victories deserve acknowledgment.

The journey to financial freedom is filled with challenges, learning curves, and moments of triumph. In Chapter 17, we celebrate the hard work, discipline, and dedication you've invested in securing your financial future. From the initial steps of creating a budget to the more advanced strategies of investing and retirement planning, each achievement contributes to your overall financial success.

This chapter explores the importance of setting and celebrating financial milestones. By breaking down larger financial objectives into manageable goals, you not only make progress more tangible but also provide yourself with more opportunities to savor success. We delve into the psychology of accomplishment, emphasizing how positive reinforcement can reinforce good financial habits and inspire further achievements.

Moreover, Chapter 17 encourages you to share your financial successes with your support network. Whether it's friends, family, or mentors, sharing your victories creates a sense of community and allows others to celebrate with you. It's a reminder that financial success is not a solitary endeavor but a collective effort.

As you embark on this chapter, take a moment to reflect on your financial journey thus far. Celebrate the victories, acknowledge the lessons learned from challenges, and use the positive energy to propel yourself toward future financial accomplishments. Chapter 17 is your opportunity to bask in the glow of your financial triumphs and set the stage for continued success on your path to financial well-being.

Recognizing Achievements Along the Journey

In the pursuit of financial well-being, it's essential to recognize and celebrate the achievements that mark your journey. Chapter 17, Section 17.1 is dedicated to the significance of acknowledging milestones along the way. These achievements, whether big or small, serve as markers of progress, keeping you motivated and reinforcing positive financial habits.

Financial success is not a single, grand event; rather, it's a series of steps and accomplishments that accumulate over time. Section 17.1 emphasizes the importance of breaking down your financial goals into manageable tasks. By setting smaller, achievable milestones, you make your progress more tangible and, in turn, foster a sense of accomplishment.

Consider the journey to paying off a substantial debt. Instead of fixating solely on the final payment, celebrate each installment made. Recognize the sacrifices and budgeting adjustments you've made to meet these milestones. It could be as simple as a mental acknowledgment or a small celebration with your support network.

Acknowledging achievements isn't just about reveling in success; it's also a strategic move in maintaining your financial journey's momentum. Psychology plays a significant role in financial habits, and positive reinforcement is a powerful tool. When you recognize and celebrate your accomplishments, you reinforce the behavior that led to success, making it more likely to be repeated.

Moreover, Section 17.1 encourages you to share your achievements with those around you. Your support network, whether friends, family, or mentors, can provide valuable encouragement and perspective. Sharing your journey fosters a sense of community and allows your loved ones to partake in the joy of your successes.

Reflect on the financial goals you've achieved so far. Perhaps you've successfully created an emergency fund, stuck to a budget for several consecutive months, or saved for a specific purpose. Recognize the effort and discipline invested in these accomplishments. They are not mere financial transactions but markers of your dedication and commitment to securing your financial future.

As you progress through your financial journey, make it a habit to regularly pause and acknowledge your achievements. Celebrate the financial victories, learn from the challenges, and carry the positive energy forward. Section 17.1 is an invitation to embrace the journey, recognizing that every step forward is a cause for celebration on the path to lasting financial success.

REFLECTING ON PERSONAL AND FINANCIAL GROWTH

As you navigate the intricate landscape of your financial journey, it's crucial to dedicate time for introspection and self-awareness. This nuanced exploration of personal and financial growth is the focal point of this segment.

Reflecting on your personal and financial growth involves a multifaceted examination of your experiences, decisions, and the lessons derived from both successes and setbacks. This introspective process is not about dwelling on mistakes or triumphs but rather understanding the evolving nature of your relationship with money.

Consider the financial goals you set for yourself in the past. How have these aspirations changed or adapted to the shifting circumstances of your life? Reflection provides a lens through which you can analyze the alignment of your financial objectives with your current values and priorities.

Personal growth, intertwined with financial development, is often a continuous journey of self-discovery. Your attitudes toward money, spending habits, and approach to financial planning can evolve over time. This reflection allows you to discern patterns and make intentional choices in alignment with your current aspirations.

Moreover, examining your financial growth involves an honest assessment of your financial literacy. Have you acquired new knowledge and skills to enhance your understanding of money matters? Whether it's learning about investments, budgeting techniques, or understanding financial instruments, each step contributes to your financial empowerment.

One valuable aspect of this reflective process is acknowledging the challenges you've overcome. Financial journeys are rarely linear, and obstacles are inevitable. By recognizing the hurdles you've faced, you gain a profound understanding of your resilience and adaptability. These qualities are not only commendable but instrumental in facing future financial challenges with confidence.

Celebrating your successes during this reflective exercise is equally important. Acknowledge the achievements, no matter how small, as they represent intentional steps toward your financial well-being. Perhaps you've successfully negotiated a better interest rate on a loan, increased your credit score, or consistently contributed to your retirement fund. These accomplishments showcase your dedication and growing financial competence.

As you engage in this process of introspection, consider the emotional aspects tied to your financial decisions. How have your attitudes, fears, or aspirations evolved? Understanding the emotional underpinnings of your financial choices provides invaluable insights into your relationship with money.

In essence, reflecting on personal and financial growth is a holistic examination of your journey. It invites you to embrace the transformative nature of your experiences, cultivating a mindful and intentional approach to your financial future. This ongoing practice of self-awareness positions you to make informed, empowered decisions, fostering a balanced and prosperous life.

SETTING NEW GOALS FOR CONTINUED SUCCESS

Embarking on the journey of setting new goals for continued success is an invigorating phase of your financial evolution. As you reflect on your achievements and learnings, the process of goal-setting becomes a dynamic tool for shaping the next chapter of your financial story.

Setting new goals is not just about the destination; it's about the transformative power of the journey. Consider what truly matters to you at this juncture of your life. Your goals should be aligned with your evolving values, aspirations, and the lessons garnered from your financial history.

Begin by envisioning your ideal financial future. What does financial success look like for you? Whether it's achieving a significant savings milestone, eliminating debt, or making substantial progress in your investments, this vision forms the foundation of your new goals. Embrace the opportunity to dream big while ensuring your goals are realistic and attainable.

Reflect on the lessons learned from past goals. What worked well, and what could be improved? This introspective analysis helps refine your goal-setting strategy, allowing for more informed and effective decisions. It's an opportunity to build on your strengths and address any challenges encountered in the pursuit of previous objectives.

In the realm of financial goals, diversification is key. Consider setting goals in various aspects of your financial life, such as savings, investments, debt reduction, and education. This diversified approach ensures a holistic and balanced advancement toward overall financial well-being.

The SMART criteria—Specific, Measurable, Achievable, Relevant, and Time-bound—serve as a valuable guide in crafting well-defined goals. Specificity clarifies the objective, measurability provides a clear benchmark for success, achievability ensures a realistic pursuit, relevance aligns with your overall vision, and time-bound sets a deadline for achievement.

Moreover, consider incorporating both short-term and long-term goals into your financial blueprint. Short-term goals offer a sense of immediacy and accomplishment, while long-term goals provide a broader perspective and a roadmap for sustained success.

As you set new goals, factor in the dynamic nature of life. Be open to adapting your goals as circumstances change. Flexibility in goal-setting allows for a responsive and resilient financial strategy, ensuring that your aspirations remain aligned with the ever-evolving landscape of your life.

Celebrate the act of setting goals as a commitment to your continued growth and prosperity. This process is not only a roadmap for financial success but also a testament to your dedication to crafting a life of purpose and fulfillment. Each goal becomes a stepping stone, propelling you forward on your journey to financial well-being and beyond.

Paying It Forward

Paying it forward is a powerful and rewarding concept that goes beyond personal financial success. It involves sharing your knowledge, resources, and experiences to uplift others on their journeys to financial well-being. As you celebrate your achievements, consider the profound impact you can have by extending a helping hand to those around you.

One of the most impactful ways to pay it forward is by sharing your financial knowledge. Offer guidance and insights to friends, family, or colleagues who may be navigating similar financial challenges. Whether it's providing budgeting tips, explaining investment strategies, or sharing lessons learned from your own experiences, your wisdom can serve as a valuable resource for others seeking to enhance their financial literacy.

Mentorship is another meaningful avenue for paying it forward. Consider becoming a mentor to someone who is just starting their career or financial journey. Your guidance and support can provide them with valuable perspectives, helping them make informed decisions and avoid potential pitfalls. The mentor-mentee relationship is a two-way street, fostering growth and learning for both parties involved.

Volunteering your time and expertise with organizations focused on financial education and empowerment is a tangible way to make a positive impact in your community. Many

non-profit organizations and community groups offer programs designed to enhance financial literacy, and your participation can contribute to building a more financially resilient
community.

Financial support, when possible, is a direct and impactful
way to pay it forward. This could involve assisting a friend in
need, contributing to a charitable cause, or supporting initiatives that align with your values. Acts of kindness, no matter
how small, can create a ripple effect, inspiring others to do
the same.

In addition to individual efforts, consider advocating for
broader changes that promote financial inclusivity and well-
being. Support policies and initiatives that aim to address
systemic issues related to financial inequality. Your voice,
combined with others, can contribute to creating a more equitable financial landscape for everyone.

Remember that paying it forward extends beyond financial
matters. Acts of kindness, empathy, and encouragement can
have a profound impact on someone's life. Whether it's offering emotional support during challenging times or celebrating
the successes of those around you, these gestures contribute
to fostering a positive and supportive community.

As you pay it forward, recognize that your actions contribute to a collective effort to create a more compassionate
and resilient society. Your commitment to making a positive
impact can inspire a chain reaction, where the generosity and
goodwill you extend to others become catalysts for positive
change in the lives of many. By embracing the spirit of paying
it forward, you become an integral part of building a community that thrives on shared success and mutual support.

MENTORING OTHER MOMS

Mentoring other moms is a profoundly impactful way to
pay it forward and contribute to the collective strength of

mothers in the journey towards financial well-being. The challenges and triumphs that come with managing family finances are universal, making the guidance and support from someone who has navigated similar waters especially valuable.

When you choose to mentor other moms, you're not just sharing financial advice – you're creating a connection built on shared experiences. Many mothers face unique financial challenges, from balancing the demands of parenthood to navigating career choices that align with family needs. By offering your insights, you can help them navigate these complexities with greater confidence.

Begin by cultivating an open and non-judgmental space for conversations. Financial matters can be sensitive, and creating an environment where other moms feel comfortable sharing their concerns and aspirations is crucial. Share your own experiences transparently, emphasizing that everyone's journey is unique, and there's no one-size-fits-all approach to financial success.

Listen actively to understand their specific challenges and goals. Effective mentoring involves a two-way exchange of ideas and experiences. By actively listening, you can tailor your guidance to address their individual needs, ensuring that your advice is not only relevant but also meaningful in their context.

Empower them with knowledge and practical skills. Financial literacy is a key component of financial empowerment. Provide resources and information on budgeting, saving, investing, and other essential financial concepts. Equip them with the tools they need to make informed decisions for their families' financial well-being.

Encourage goal-setting and planning. Help other moms articulate their financial goals and develop a roadmap to achieve them. Whether it's saving for education, homeownership, or retirement, assisting them in setting realistic and achievable goals can instill a sense of purpose and direction in their financial journey.

Share networking opportunities and resources. Building a supportive community is crucial for moms seeking financial empowerment. Introduce them to relevant networks, online communities, or local groups where they can connect with other moms facing similar challenges. Networking can provide emotional support and open doors to valuable opportunities.

Provide ongoing support and encouragement. The journey to financial well-being is often filled with ups and downs. Offer continuous support, celebrating their successes and providing encouragement during challenging times. A mentor's role extends beyond the transmission of knowledge – it involves being a steadfast supporter and cheerleader.

Lead by example. Demonstrate the principles of financial responsibility in your own life. Your actions speak louder than words, and seeing your commitment to sound financial practices can be inspiring for those you mentor. Share stories of your own financial journey, emphasizing the lessons you've learned along the way.

Ultimately, mentoring other moms is a reciprocal and transformative experience. As you share your wisdom and guidance, you also gain insights from their unique perspectives. The bond forged through mentorship contributes not only to individual growth but also to the strengthening of a community where moms uplift and empower each other in their pursuit of financial well-being.

BUILDING A SUPPORTIVE FINANCIAL COMMUNITY

Building a supportive financial community is a powerful and essential aspect of fostering collective growth and empowerment. In the intricate tapestry of personal finance, the strength of a community lies not only in shared knowledge but also in the mutual support that propels each member towards their financial goals.

One of the cornerstones of a supportive financial community is open communication. Establishing a platform or a space where members can freely discuss their financial journeys, share challenges, and celebrate successes creates an environment of trust and understanding. This open dialogue fosters a sense of camaraderie, reminding everyone that they are not alone in facing financial hurdles.

Encourage a culture of empathy and non-judgment within the community. Recognize that each member has a unique set of circumstances, challenges, and goals. By promoting understanding and compassion, you create an inclusive atmosphere where everyone feels comfortable seeking advice, sharing their experiences, and offering support without fear of criticism.

Facilitate connections and networking opportunities. Building a supportive financial community is not just about sharing advice; it's also about creating meaningful connections. Provide avenues for community members to connect with others who share similar financial goals or have overcome similar challenges. Networking can lead to valuable collaborations, shared resources, and a broader support system.

Celebrate diversity within the community. Recognize that financial goals and challenges differ based on factors such as family structure, career choices, and cultural background. Embrace and celebrate this diversity as a source of strength. Encourage members to share their unique perspectives, allowing the community to benefit from a rich tapestry of experiences.

Offer educational resources and workshops. Empower members by providing access to financial education resources and hosting workshops on relevant topics. A well-informed community is better equipped to make sound financial decisions. Whether it's budgeting, investing, or planning for the future, shared knowledge enhances the collective financial literacy of the community.

Establish mentorship programs. Encourage experienced members to mentor those who are just starting their financial journeys. Mentorship not only imparts valuable insights but also creates meaningful connections within the community. The guidance provided by seasoned members can significantly impact the financial well-being of those seeking support.

Create a positive and motivating atmosphere. Infuse the community with positivity and motivation. Celebrate achievements, no matter how small, and provide words of encouragement during challenging times. A positive atmosphere contributes to a sense of optimism and resilience, crucial elements in overcoming financial obstacles.

Organize community events and activities. Foster a sense of unity by organizing events and activities that bring community members together. Whether it's a financial planning workshop, a casual meetup, or a collaborative project, these events strengthen the bonds within the community, fostering a supportive and uplifting environment.

Encourage accountability and goal tracking. Implement mechanisms that encourage members to set financial goals, track their progress, and be accountable to the community. Shared accountability creates a sense of responsibility and commitment, motivating members to stay on course and actively contribute to the collective success of the community.

In conclusion, building a supportive financial community is a dynamic and ongoing process that requires active participation, open communication, and a genuine commitment to each member's success. By creating an environment where individuals feel heard, understood, and supported, you contribute to the collective strength and resilience of the community on its journey towards financial well-being.

Chapter 18

Chapter 18:
Conclusion

As we reach the final chapter of this comprehensive guide, it's time to reflect on the incredible journey we've embarked on together. Throughout this book, we've explored the vast landscape of personal finance, delving into the nuances of budgeting, saving, investing, and building a secure financial future. Now, in Chapter 18, we bring our exploration to a close with a sense of accomplishment, armed with newfound knowledge and empowered with practical strategies.

The essence of this guide has been more than a mere compilation of financial advice; it has been a companion on your unique financial journey. Whether you're a seasoned financial veteran or someone just starting to navigate the intricate realm of personal finance, the insights shared within these pages have aimed to provide clarity, guidance, and a friendly hand to guide you through the maze of financial decision-making.

Throughout the chapters, we've discussed the importance of setting realistic goals, understanding government assistance programs, navigating insurance and protection, planning for your children's education, building a support network, exploring entrepreneurship, preparing for retirement, and much more. Each section has been crafted with care, offering practical advice and friendly encouragement to help you navigate the diverse challenges that may arise on your financial path.

As we approach the conclusion, take a moment to celebrate your achievements, whether big or small, and appreciate the progress you've made. Personal finance is a journey, not a destination, and the lessons learned here are designed to serve you well as you continue to grow and adapt to life's ever-changing circumstances.

In Chapter 18, we'll recap some key takeaways, reinforcing the principles that form the foundation of a sound financial strategy. We'll also explore the concept of financial wellness and how it extends beyond mere monetary concerns to encompass your overall well-being. Consider this chapter a reflection on the knowledge gained and an invitation to carry the momentum forward as you shape your financial future.

So, let's embark on this final chapter together, cherishing the lessons learned, celebrating the progress made, and looking ahead with confidence and optimism. Your financial journey is uniquely yours, and this conclusion is not an endpoint but a stepping stone to continued growth, resilience, and financial well-being.

The Ongoing Pursuit of Financial Freedom

In the grand tapestry of personal finance, the pursuit of financial freedom is not a one-time event but a continuous journey, a melody that plays throughout the various stages of our lives. As we delve into the essence of ongoing financial freedom in this section, let's explore the dynamic nature of our relationship with money and how our understanding evolves over time.

Financial freedom is not a fixed destination but a flexible concept that adapts to the ebb and flow of life. It's not solely about accumulating wealth but embracing a mindset that allows you to make intentional choices aligned with your values and aspirations. The journey involves a perpetual cycle of setting goals, making informed decisions, and adjusting course as circumstances evolve.

One key aspect of this ongoing pursuit is the ability to adapt to changes. Life is unpredictable, and your financial plan should reflect this reality. Whether it's a career shift, a family milestone, or unforeseen challenges, your financial strategy should be nimble enough to accommodate these shifts. This adaptability ensures that your pursuit of financial freedom remains resilient in the face of life's twists and turns.

Another integral component is the cultivation of financial wellness. Beyond the numbers on a balance sheet, financial wellness encompasses your overall well-being. It's about striking a harmonious balance between your financial, physical, and mental health. Regularly assess your goals, reassess your priorities, and consider how your financial decisions contribute to your holistic well-being.

As you navigate this ongoing journey, remember the importance of education. Stay informed about financial trends, investment options, and evolving economic landscapes. Continuous learning equips you with the knowledge needed to make informed decisions, empowering you to adapt to changing circumstances with confidence.

A crucial part of the ongoing pursuit of financial freedom is also celebrating your victories, no matter how small. Acknowledge the progress you make, applaud the milestones achieved, and use these moments as motivation to propel you forward. Positive reinforcement reinforces the habits that contribute to your financial well-being.

Lastly, remember that financial freedom is not a solo endeavor. Building a supportive network, seeking guidance from mentors, and sharing insights with others can enhance your journey. Collaboration and shared experiences create a robust foundation for sustained financial success.

In conclusion, the ongoing pursuit of financial freedom is a symphony that requires continuous effort, adaptability, and a holistic approach to well-being. As you progress along this journey, embrace the evolving nature of your financial landscape, celebrating the milestones, learning from challenges, and maintaining a resilient spirit that propels you toward a future of sustained financial well-being.

EMBRACING A LIFELONG LEARNING MINDSET

Embracing a lifelong learning mindset is akin to opening a window to a world of continual growth, discovery, and personal development. In the context of your ongoing pursuit of financial freedom, adopting this mindset becomes a powerful catalyst for navigating the ever-evolving landscape of personal finance.

Picture your financial journey as a vibrant ecosystem, where knowledge is the sunlight that nurtures growth. Just as the financial world undergoes constant transformations, so should your understanding and awareness. A lifelong learning mindset is the key that unlocks the door to this treasury of knowledge.

Start by acknowledging that learning is not confined to classrooms or textbooks. The world around you is a rich source of insights waiting to be tapped. Stay curious and cultivate a habit of asking questions. Whether it's understanding the nuances of investment strategies, exploring new avenues of income generation, or deciphering complex financial jargon, curiosity is your compass.

The digital age has bestowed upon us a treasure trove of educational resources. From online courses and webinars to podcasts and articles, there's an abundance of information at your fingertips. Take advantage of these resources to deepen your financial literacy. Engage with diverse perspectives, and don't shy away from tackling topics that might initially seem intimidating.

Mistakes are stepping stones on the path to mastery. Approach your financial journey with a growth mindset, recognizing that every misstep is an opportunity to learn and refine your approach. Whether it's a less-than-ideal investment or a financial decision that didn't pan out as expected, view these moments as valuable lessons that contribute to your financial acumen.

Networking is another facet of lifelong learning. Surround yourself with individuals who inspire and challenge you. Seek out mentors who have navigated similar financial waters and learn from their experiences. Engaging in discussions with peers, attending financial seminars, and participating in online forums can broaden your perspectives and expose you to a wealth of collective wisdom.

Moreover, be open to unlearning and relearning. The financial landscape is dynamic, and what worked yesterday may not be applicable tomorrow. Embrace change with a sense of curiosity and adaptability. Continuous learning requires a certain level of humility—the acknowledgment that there is always more to discover and understand.

In the realm of personal finance, technology is a powerful ally. Stay abreast of technological advancements that can streamline your financial management, from budgeting apps to investment platforms. Embracing technological tools not only enhances efficiency but also empowers you to make more informed decisions in the digital age.

In essence, embracing a lifelong learning mindset is about fostering intellectual agility and adaptability. It's an acknowledgment that the journey to financial freedom is a dynamic, ever-evolving expedition. By staying curious, learning from diverse sources, and being open to change, you equip yourself with the tools needed to navigate the complexities of personal finance and ensure a prosperous and fulfilling financial journey.

CONTINUING THE JOURNEY TO EMPOWERED FINANCES

Continuing the journey to empowered finances is a celebration of resilience, growth, and the unwavering spirit that propels you forward on your quest for financial well-being. As you stand at the threshold of this concluding section, reflect on the transformative odyssey you've undertaken, marked by a commitment to understanding, adapting, and thriving in the dynamic world of personal finance.

The journey to empowered finances is a testament to your capacity for growth and learning. It's an acknowledgment that every financial decision, whether triumphant or challenging, contributes to your evolution. Each step you've taken has been a stride toward a more empowered and informed version of yourself. The knowledge you've gained, the skills you've honed, and the experiences you've embraced have collectively woven a tapestry of financial wisdom.

Consider the challenges you've encountered not as obstacles but as stepping stones, guiding you toward a future defined by financial mastery. Life's unpredictability may have thrown curveballs your way, but your resilience and ability to navigate turbulent waters have fortified you. The journey is not about avoiding storms but about learning to dance in the rain, emerging stronger and more resilient after each downpour.

Empowered finances are a reflection of your values and aspirations. They encapsulate not just monetary success but the holistic well-being of your life. Your financial journey is intertwined with your dreams, passions, and the profound connections you forge with family and community. It's a dynamic tapestry that extends beyond spreadsheets and bank statements, encompassing the richness of a life well-lived.

As you continue this journey, remember the importance of balance. While financial success is a worthy pursuit, it should be harmonized with your overall well-being. Cherish moments of joy, cultivate meaningful relationships, and savor the experiences that make life extraordinary. Empowered finances are a means to an end – the end being a life imbued with purpose, fulfillment, and genuine happiness.

In the realm of personal finance, empowerment is a perpetual process rather than a finite destination. The financial world will continue to evolve, and with it, so will your strategies and insights. Stay committed to the principles of lifelong learning and adaptability. Embrace change as an opportunity for growth, and let curiosity be your guide as you navigate the ever-shifting landscapes of finance and life.

Finally, pay it forward. Share your knowledge, experiences, and insights with others embarking on their financial journeys. Be a beacon of inspiration and support for fellow moms and individuals striving for financial empowerment. As you illuminate their paths, you reinforce your own commitment to lifelong learning and the enduring pursuit of financial freedom.

Your journey to empowered finances is not just a solitary endeavor; it's a collective movement toward a brighter and more prosperous future for yourself, your family, and the community you touch. So, as you step into the next chapter of your life, carry with you the lessons, the resilience, and the empowered spirit that has defined this transformative journey. Here's to a future of continued growth, fulfillment, and financial prosperity!